God in Action

Problems in Theology

God in Action
A Reader

Edited by
Jeff Astley, David Brown and Ann Loades

T & T CLARK INTERNATIONAL
A Continuum imprint
LONDON • NEW YORK

T & T CLARK INTERNATIONAL LTD
A Continuum imprint

The Tower Building   15 East 26th Street
11 York Road   New York, NY 10010
London SE1 7NX, UK   USA

www.tandtclark.com

Copyright © T & T Clark International Ltd, 2004

British Library Cataloguing-in-Publication Data
A catalogue record for this book is available from the British Library

ISBN 0 567 082 237 (paperback)
ISBN 0 567 082 334 (hardback)

Typeset by RefineCatch Limited, Bungay, Suffolk
Printed and bound in Great Britain by
MPG Books Ltd, Bodmin, Cornwall

Contents

Contents

Preface

Courses in theology and religious studies in universities, colleges and sixth forms are increasingly 'topic-based' or 'problem-based', and usually form part of modular programmes of study for first degrees or AS/A2 level qualifications. Teachers and students often find it difficult to access relevant primary material for the different topics that they have selected to study. Many textbooks are too general to be of more than limited value, and the same is true of selections of readings.

This series of readers in *Problems in Theology* is designed to meet this need by focusing on particular controversial themes and issues. Each volume provides a set of carefully selected readings from primary sources, together with a brief introductory essay, topics for discussion or further study, and a select bibliography. A particular advantage of the format adopted here is that teachers and students can use the material selectively, constructing their own educational pathway through a problem.

The readings chosen for these books have been tested out with undergraduate classes in the University of Durham and elsewhere. Much of this material will also be accessible, however, to sixth form students of religious studies, as well as to those studying theology on ordination courses and in adult and continuing education.

The editors wish to thank all who have assisted in this project by helping in the selection, referencing and trial-testing of material, by copy-typing and editing the text, or by securing permissions. Particular thanks go to Brad Embry, Evelyn Jackson, Paul Murray and Declan O'Sullivan.

Notes on the text

The passages are printed (except for omissions, indicated by three full stops) as in the original text, with the same spelling, punctuation etc. In most cases, however, notes within the readings have been omitted.

From time to time the editors have added their own explanatory comments. These are printed in italics and enclosed in square brackets.

Introduction

Reading the readings

The claim that God has acted and now acts 'in' or 'towards' the world would seem to be central to the Christian faith. It used to be fashionable, indeed, to describe the Bible as the 'Book of the Acts of God', and the biblical material that recounts God's activity ranks among the most striking of its contents (see Readings 1.1, 2.1, 3.1, 4.1). Nevertheless, since the eighteenth-century Enlightenment at least, divine action has been one of the most controversial topics in Christian theology.

Disagreements over nomenclature and definition have often clouded discussion in this area, but most writers have distinguished the activity of God in originally creating and continuing to sustain the universe in being, from the categories of general and special (or particular) providence and of miracle (see Michael Langford, in 1.2).[1] For many, this list – often with the addition of the Incarnation of God in Christ – reveals a series of types of divine activity that reflects increasing degrees of God's involvement with the universe, even of 'intervention'. Here the debate gets most intense, with a polarization between those who want to collapse the distinctive categories of divine action into one, understood 'in relation to the world as a whole rather than to particular occurrences within it' (Maurice Wiles, in 1.2), and those who identify particular events rather than others as 'acts of God', perhaps with reference to whether they can be said to fulfil God's intentions (cf. Vincent Brümmer, in 1.2).[2]

Related debates concern the metaphors or models that may be employed to speak of God's activity of caring and control within the created realm. Is God best thought of as a clockmaker or other artisan, or

[1] On God's initial creation and continuing preservation of the world, see Jeff Astley, David Brown and Ann Loades (eds), *Creation: A Reader*, London, T & T Clark, 2003.

[2] The physical and biological sciences inevitably raise other questions about God's relationship to the natural world. See Jeff Astley, David Brown and Ann Loades (eds), *Science and Religion: A Reader*, London, T & T Clark International, 2004.

an author or artist; as a speaker in a relationship of dialogue, or as a king
or parent (see 1.4, 1.5 and Keith Ward in 2.2)? Having adopted the right
image, how should we then think of God's responsibility for evil and his
relationship to the free actions of human beings (cf. 1.4)?[3]

For traditional believers, the theological (and devotional) shoe is likely
to pinch most severely when they consider the possibility of miraculous
divine action. Miracles are often perceived as extreme examples of particular providence that only occur when God overrides the natural order.
This would seem to fit such biblical examples as the parting of the Red
Sea (Exodus 14), the 'nature miracles' of Jesus and, in the view of many,
his miracles of healing (see 2.1). Whereas God's normal providential care
is sometimes pictured using the image of a person steering a boat this
way or that down a river, within the defined limits of the river banks, in
the case of a miracle 'the boatman' steers the boat out of the river
altogether, transcending the boundaries of the known laws of nature by
an action that is analogous to transporting the vessel across dry land.
Miraculous events are therefore not only unexpected and anomalous,
by comparison with the normal run of cause and effect in nature, but in
principle unpredictable. Too many examples of such events would, of
course, undermine the very notion of a reliable order of nature; too few,
however, lays God open to the charge of favouritism and exacerbates the
problem of evil (see David Jenkins, in 2.3; cf. also Helen Oppenheimer, in
1.2 and Stewart Sutherland, in 4.4).

Resisting this tendency to define miracles as 'violations of the usual
course of nature', a definition that David Hume encouraged to good
sceptical effect (2.4), others have argued that their key feature is rather
that they are religiously (and/or morally) significant events. To call
something a miracle, on this view, is to imply that it gives rise to religious
awe, wonder and gratitude (2.2, 2.3). Some, including Paul Tillich (in 2.2)
and Friedrich Schleiermacher,[4] emphasize this religious element at the
expense of the element of scientific inexplicability. Although this strategy
allows a wide-ranging spirituality that finds God's hand everywhere, the
word 'miracle' might seem to lose its point unless we can distinguish
some events as not being miraculous.

A number of theological problems that cluster around the notions
of providence and miracle come into clear focus in discussing answers to

---

[3] See Jeff Astley, David Brown and Ann Loades (eds), *Evil: A Reader*, London,
T & T Clark, 2003.

[4] 'Miracle is simply the religious name for event. . . . The more religious you are, the
more miracle would you see everywhere' (Friedrich Schleiermacher, *On Religion*,
ET New York, Harper & Row, 1958, p. 88).

prayer. Believers often speak of God as responding to prayer either by strengthening the concern of the person who prays, and her determination to act on the basis of that concern, or by helping her to accept whatever happens as God's will (cf. 3.5). We may wonder, however, whether God is needed to effect such spiritual or psychological 'answers'. Yet if 'our asking in faith may make it possible for God to do something which he could not have done without our asking' (Peter Baelz, in 3.3), how is this process best conceived? The additional effect has commonly been understood in terms of God's providential activity or miraculous intervention, but the usual problems then arise – together with some new ones (3.4). There are, we should note, less traditional options to be considered (see H. H. Price and Fraser Watts, in 3.3).

All such discussion needs to bear in mind both that praying for things is only a part of prayer (cf. 3.1), and that prayer should always be explored primarily in terms of its spiritual significance, rather than as a location for intellectual debates. God's activity and nature will be construed in very different ways depending on a person's experience of and in prayer (cf. 3.2, 3.5, 3.6).

Eleonore Stump contends that the great value of making prayerful requests is that they allow us to have a relationship with God that neither spoils nor dominates us.[5] This wider religious, spiritual and devotional context is also highly relevant to those discussions in which God's action is understood in terms of grace. Here we can do no more than sample some aspects of this historically contentious doctrine. Grace is expressed in Scripture in terms of a profoundly personal relationship (4.1), and recent writers in this area tend to favour this personal dimension (4.3, 4.4) rather than the mediaeval notion of grace as an impersonal created thing. This emphasis needs to be borne in mind when considering the early debates over grace and freedom (4.2), as well as the wider theological literature on the nature, context and forms of grace which includes the Reformation debate over our 'justification' by God's grace, concerning which there is now much more common ground (4.5).[6] For many, the theology of grace is best approached through a consideration of human experience (cf. 4.3).

[5] Eleonore Stump and Michael J. Murray (eds), *Philosophy of Religion: The Big Questions*, Oxford, Blackwell, 1999, pp. 353–66.
[6] See Anthony N. S. Lane, *Justification by Faith in Catholic-Protestant Dialogue*, London, T & T Clark, 2002.

1 Providence

1.1 Providence in the Bible

Genesis 12:1–3

12 ¹Now the LORD said to Abram, 'Go from your country and your kindred and your father's house to the land that I will show you. ²I will make of you a great nation, and I will bless you, and make your name great, so that you will be a blessing. ³I will bless those who bless you, and the one who curses you I will curse; and in you all the families of the earth shall be blessed.'

Genesis 45:4–8

45 ⁴Then Joseph said to his brothers, 'Come closer to me.' And they came closer. He said, 'I am your brother Joseph, whom you sold into Egypt. ⁵And now do not be distressed, or angry with yourselves, because you sold me here; for God sent me before you to preserve life. ⁶For the famine has been in the land these two years; and there are five more years in which there will be neither ploughing nor harvest. ⁷God sent me before you to preserve for you a remnant on earth, and to keep alive for you many survivors. ⁸So it was not you who sent me here, but God; he has made me a father to Pharaoh, and lord of all his house and ruler over all the land of Egypt.'

Matthew 6:26–30

6 ²⁶'Look at the birds of the air; they neither sow nor reap nor gather into barns, and yet your heavenly Father feeds them. Are you not of more value than they? ²⁷And can any of you by worrying add a single hour to your span of life? ²⁸And why do you worry about clothing? Consider the lilies of the field, how they grow; they neither toil nor spin, ²⁹yet I tell you, even Solomon in all his glory was not clothed like one of these. ³⁰But if God so clothes the grass of the field, which is alive today and tomorrow is thrown into the oven, will he not much more clothe you – you of little faith?'

Philippians 2:12–13

2 ^{12}Therefore, my beloved, just as you have always obeyed me, not only in my presence, but much more now in my absence, work out your own salvation with fear and trembling; ^{13}for it is God who is at work in you, enabling you both to will and to work for his good pleasure.

1.2 Locating God's action

Helen Oppenheimer, *Finding and Following,* London, SCM, 1994, pp. 49–51, 54–5

Being grateful to God for good fortune begins to go wrong if there is a lurking idea that the people who are not so blessed are somehow or other less dear to God. Gratitude slips easily into smugness. 'The heart is deceitful above all things, and desperately wicked' (Jeremiah 17:9). That is a strong way of pointing out that human virtue is particularly prone to topple over into self-deception. Good people begin to take themselves too seriously and nobody is brave enough, or unkind enough, to argue or mock them out of it.

To undermine somebody else's confidence is a failure of charity. When people are bearing witness to what they themselves have found to make them grateful they should be heard, not snubbed. But also, people must be allowed and encouraged to be honest about what they have not found. Christians ought not to let themselves slip into the kind of mechanical thankfulness which invites the reaction, 'You would say that whatever happened.'

There are difficulties in theory and in practice about the notion of God continually intervening in response to faithful prayers. Christians who keep looking out for everyday providences do not know what they ask. Unless God the Creator relinquished that kind of close control, the physical world would have to be very different from the dependable reality it is. . . .

Trust in providence is easily trivialized. 'Please, Lord, send us a fine day for the church fête.' Simple favouritism would hardly be worthy of God. Most of us have outgrown, 'Please let our team win.' It is harder to outgrow the traffic jam prayer, *'Please* let me get there in time'; but in a cool hour we know that if the lights have all turned green for us we have been lucky, not holy. It is said that 'the devil looks after his own'; but God, in that straightforward sense, obviously does not. People who think they are meant to have a helpline to heaven often have discouraging difficulties in getting through. Even if it were right for the world to be run for the benefit of the devout, the world is not run for the benefit of the devout.

A small aircraft crashes on a motorway, hitting two cars. Nobody is dangerously hurt and someone remarks, 'God must have been looking after them.' The next day a bomb explodes in Florence, killing a whole family. Whatever place can be found for this in God's ultimate purpose, it would be monstrous to suggest that God was too busy looking after some of the greatest pictures in the world to protect the human beings. It is more seemly, and more consistent with Christian faith, to reserve judgment about these emergencies and put them alongside the deaths of 'those eighteen upon whom the tower in Siloam fell and killed them' (Luke 13:4), for which the Lord had no easy explanation to give.

The main reason for being cautious about identifying providence everywhere is that the examples believers so gladly give of little providences are insensitive, in the light of other believers' sorrowful experience of their heartfelt prayers seemingly remaining unanswered. People ask God for protection against danger; they beg for healing and health; and God gives no sign.

Death, premature and pointless, does not belong only to bad old days.

. . .

It would be perverse to deny that the Bible, Hebrew and Christian, is full of belief in providence. Just so: the biblical writers are indeed bearing witness to what they themselves have found. What they tell is what they have experienced. The story is complex but the gist of it is that the God of Abraham, Isaac and Jacob is a faithful God, who sets particular individuals particular tasks, who has led the people out of Egypt, made a Covenant with them, given them a Law to live by, borne with their backslidings and constantly intervened to save them: decisively, Christians say, in Jesus Christ.

What God decides to do is characteristically different from what human beings expect. God is not to be stereotyped. To take God's policies for granted cannot be the right way to show faithful trust. It is tempting to play safe, acknowledge God's blessings of old, and simply stop looking for providence except in the past. Is it good enough to recognize and declare God's long-ago mercies to the Chosen People, and put aside assurances for individuals in the present and the future?

At least believers should be in less of a hurry to explain all everyday happenings in terms of divine care. It is all very well to say, 'I have been young, and now am old: and yet saw I never the righteous forsaken' (Psalm 37:25), but such sunny optimism is not borne out in general by human life, by the biblical record, nor by the experience of the Lord himself (Matthew 28:46; Mark 15:34). St Augustine was perplexed by this psalm. He feared, not without reason, that someone might 'be inwardly scandalized, and ask, "Is what I have chanted really true? . . . the Scriptures play us false".'

. . .

Everyday life gives good reason, and Hebrew and Christian scriptures give good authority, for refusing to presume upon special providences. Since we are responsible for one another, arousing unfounded hopes can be as much a failure of charity as discouraging cherished hopes. There is scope for being tentative, for looking at what the world is really like. When we look, we find a mixture: what matters is to get the emphasis right. The present argument is offered as a corrective to glibness, not as a counterblast to gratitude.

The idea that if people are good they can expect God to arrange things for them needs correcting because it is unrealistic and therefore cruel. Simple faith does not have to be like that, neither the simple faith of Jesus nor simple faith in Jesus. It is false to suggest that God's children have only to say their prayers and Jesus will see that everything comes right. From the psalmists and prophets onwards, religious people have often had to understand that the world does not accommodate itself even to their pious hopes.

People who have taken providence for granted have found out the hard way that providence does not mean what they thought. When Christians find themselves and the whole universe 'groaning in travail' (Romans 8:22), it is more responsible to tell them to read the Book of Job than to tell them to rely on providence here and now. It was Job's comforters, not Job, who were convinced that his troubles were all for the best.

Michael J. Langford, *Providence*, London, SCM, 1981, pp. 5–6, 11–14, 17–18

If I am the leader and guide of a climbing party, there are at least three ways in which I can control events. First, in the initial planning of the expedition, such as the selection of suitable ropes and maps. Second, in the day-by-day leading of the party, perhaps by going first as we climb a rock face. Third, by occasional *ad hoc* decisions, made on the spur of the moment, as I deal with emergencies when they arise. This third kind of leadership may be predictable in general, in that it is certain that I shall have to deal with the unexpected, and that the kind of action that I am likely to take may be known from my character, but unpredictable in detail.

If we use this example as a crude model for divine guidance in the world, we find that it must be expanded to a sixfold model. Divine guidance or government can refer to at least six kinds of activity, although it will be obvious that these activities overlap. I list them as they reflect increasing involvement in the created order:

(i)   The creative activity of God.
(ii)   The sustaining activity of God.
       (These two categories together correspond with the first, or planning, stage of the climbing party model.)
(iii) God's action as final cause.
       [*A 'final cause' is something's purpose, the end towards which it is directed and for the sake of which it occurs.*]
(iv)   The activity known as general providence.
       (These two categories together correspond with the second stage of the climbing party model. The emphasis is neither on prior planning nor on individual decisions, but on the smooth and predictable running of an enterprise.)
(v)   The activity known as special providence.
(vi)   The miraculous.
       (These two categories together correspond to the *ad hoc* decisions and actions made by the party leader.)

All six of these categories can refer to the activity of God, and therefore in the broadest sense all can be taken as aspects of providence. Most of the time, however, we do not find it helpful to use words in too broad a sense, and the custom has developed, for good reasons, of contrasting one kind of divine activity with another. My own suggestion is that in most contexts we restrict the use of the word 'providence' to categories four and five, and that on many occasions it is also helpful to make the further distinction between general and special providence.

. . .

(iv) *General providence*. Not all the important writers on providence make an explicit distinction between general and special providence. Aquinas, for example, includes both ideas under his overall account of providence. The distinction, however, is useful; and when it is not made, it is often possible to detect two different emphases in a writer's thought.

General providence refers to the government of the universe through the universal laws that control or influence nature, man, and history, without the need for specific or *ad hoc* acts of divine will. Sometimes it is hard to distinguish this notion from that of creation, when that concept is thought of as a continuing activity, or from the notion of final causality; nevertheless there are differences. General providence suggests a planner who watches over and influences the general evolution of the universe, whereas the first three notions that I have discussed could be held to be compatible with a God who is unaware of, or uninterested in, the actual evolution of things. Indeed, there have been philosophies of religion that have advocated belief in such a God. However, although the notion of general providence suggests some sort of intelligent plan and oversight, this need not involve concern for individual human beings, and it does not necessarily imply what most people would regard as a 'personal' God. A personal God, as I shall attempt to show, is bound up with the notion of special providence.

A typical description of the idea of general providence is given by William Sherlock, Dean of St Paul's Cathedral in the late seventeenth century, and a well known apologist in his day. He writes: 'The ordinary government of nature does not signify to act without it, or to over-rule its powers, but to steer and guide its motions, to serve the wise ends of his Providence in the government of mankind.'

The stress here is on the general run of nature or, correspondingly, on the general movement of history. The provision of rain, for example, which enables human beings to survive, and which falls on the just and on the unjust in a fairly predictable fashion, would be an example of general providence, but the arrival of rain in the middle of a drought in response to prayer would not be. It is this kind of general providence, perhaps to be likened to a long-term pressure on natural things to conform to a certain pattern, that lies behind religious interpretations of biological evolution, except when these interpretations depend on special mutations resulting from a more direct form of divine action. Again, the argument from design is usually related to this general pattern to be observed in nature, which, so the argument holds, demands the work of a master planner.

In practice, however, it can be very hard to draw a sharp line between this conception of a general providence and special providence. At the devotional level, for example, ought we to praise God for answering our prayers when there is a 'providential' break in the drought, or ought we to praise him for his general gift of rain, which, for all we know, may just have happened to come at this time? More significantly, from the point of view of this study, this devotional question reflects a theoretical difficulty that arises over the distinction. If general providence is concerned with the species, as is the view of some thinkers, as opposed to individuals, there is already the suggestion of some special act of will; for the species is being treated differently from the rest of the biological universe if it is in any way the object of concern as a species.

This last point can be illustrated by reference to the interesting account of providence given by the great Jewish thinker, Maimonides, in the twelfth century. He carefully distinguishes five theories of the nature of providence (*inaya*). Among the views that he rejects is that of the Islamic sect known as *Ash 'ariyya*, who held that every event was directly under the hand of providence. This is the view that I shall refer to as 'universal providence', and is essentially the same as the voluntarist views [*that everything that happens is a new creative act of God*] ... Maimonides goes on to advocate a modified version of Aristotle, in which providence does extend below the level of the moon, and is concerned with human individuals (contrary to Aristotle), but does not extend to individuals of other species. Providence has no interest in flies or blades of grass, he says, for these are entirely ordered by chance so far as individual events go. In human affairs, however, since God always acts justly, rewards and punishments are entirely controlled by God.

. . .

I hold that there is a difference between typical cases of what a Christian would call general providence, such as the steering of evolution towards creatures with larger and larger brains, and typical cases of what he would call special providence, such as the inspiration of a prophet with a special message for his people, or the answer to a particular prayer. The chief difficulty with the idea of general providence lies elsewhere: it is the problem of the apparent redundancy of the notion. It is one thing to state that God is at work in all natural processes, and another thing to explain what this claim amounts to. What is added by saying that God is at work, say, in the evolutionary process *taken as a whole*? ... If ... no difference that could be observed, even in principle, arises out of the claim that providence is at work, has anything meaningful been asserted?

(v) *Special Providence.* Some scholastics divided up providence in many more ways than I am doing, for there was providence universal, general, particular, special and most special. Such complication is unnecessary, but there is a significant distinction in human providence between the normal and predictable guidance of an enterprise, and the unpredictable and *ad hoc* decisions that may have to be made, as in the climbing party analogy. It seems reasonable to make the same distinction between two kinds of divine providence, because the biblical account of God's involvement with the world displays the same differences. God is the author of the light and the wind and the rain, as these are experienced every day, but he is also the one who speaks to the prophets and chooses Saul to be king over Israel. Special providence, as the discussion of general providence has already indicated, relates to government and guidance by specific acts, even though these acts may sometimes be of the same kind as those that general providence provides, for example, in the case of the rain that came in response to Elijah's prayer [*1 Kings 18*]. But the recipient of special providence need not be an individual, in the sense of a solitary human being, for the providential care of a group, such as Israel, would be equally significant. As we have seen, there is a problem latent here: how special must special providence be if it is not to slide into the notion of general providence? However, the root of the distinction is not the individuality of the recipient of the providential care, but the individuality of the providential act. Special providence is analogous to a human decision, and it is for this reason that it is bound up with the idea of God as personal.

A good example of the idea of special providence in the Christian tradition is given by St Augustine's *Confessions*. As Augustine looks back on his past life, he sees the hand of God manipulating particular events in order to forward the divine plan. The manipulation is both internal and external. He is guided away from Manichaean ideas in part through the desire to leave Carthage and go to Rome, a desire which Augustine sees as contrived by providence. On the way there he is hastened by suitable winds, a kind of external providential aid which his mother also enjoyed.

. . .

(vi) *The miraculous*. As we move along a line towards more obvious and invasive divine intervention in the natural order, miracles would seem to come at the end. However, even in this opening statement I have made an assertion which many Christians will disagree with. Some will not wish to make any distinction between miracle and providence, especially in the sense of special providence, and many will object strongly to the suggestion that miracles are, in any way, *interventions* in the order of nature. . . .

If one looks up the English word 'miracle' in a biblical concordance it is evident that it is used to translate words standing for a wonder, or an act of power, or a sign. There is no clear contrast with the 'order' of nature, because the very idea of an 'order' of nature, suggesting a body of inter-locking and autonomous laws, was not present. When the idea of an order of nature developed, in the modern sense, especially through thinkers such as Aquinas, it was inevitable that any account of miracle had to be interpreted to take note of this order. Aquinas' account of miracle is therefore of classic importance. He allows that in a broad sense a miracle is anything that goes beyond human capability and vision, but he insists that in the strict sense it is 'something that happens outside the whole realm of nature', and is therefore something that only God can do, not men, nor angels, nor devils. Elsewhere a further distinction is made: the acts of creation and of justifying the sinner are not, strictly speaking miracles, because they are not effects that could in any way be produced by nature, but are in a separate and still more wonderful class. Miracle refers to events produced directly by God, which in other circumstances could conceivably have been produced by nature.

Here, as all through the writings of Aquinas, we have a strong sense of the created order as having a significant autonomy. Although it ultimately depends on God as its 'first cause', it has its own 'secondary causality', which entails that it must be studied empirically for what it is. Indeed, it is hard to overestimate the importance of the stand which he took here, in opposition to many of his contemporaries, both Christian and Muslim, for the foundations of what became the modern scientific movement.

In Aquinas' account of miracle there is a clear distinction between providence and miracle, when these terms are used strictly. The former involves the guidance of the created order, the latter a sort of invasion, since any scientific explanation (in the modern sense) is ruled out as impossible in principle. . . . [T]he distinction is of great importance for the mainstream Christian tradition, for providence was indeed taken to imply a divine activity that, unlike miracle, steered nature instead of overruling it.

Maurice Wiles, *God's Action in the World*, London, SCM, 1986, pp. 28–9, 37–8, 84–5

[T]he proposal that I want to make is that the primary usage for the idea of divine action should be in relation to the world as a whole rather than to particular occurrences within it. Preliminary support for this proposal can be found in the final chapter of John Macmurray's book, *The Self as*

Agent. For he claims there that 'the only way in which we can conceive our experience as a whole is by thinking of the world as one action'. The category of action, he argues, is more fundamental than that of process. For action can incorporate process, but not the other way round. The unifying intentionality which is the distinctive and constitutive feature of 'action' cannot be fully brought within the idea of an ongoing process. 'It is therefore *possible*,' Macmurray concludes, 'to think the world as one action. It is *not possible* to think it as a unitary process' (*Self as Agent*, London, Faber & Faber, 1969, p. 220).

So for the theist, who is necessarily committed to a unitary view of the world, the whole process of the bringing into being of the world, which is still going on, needs to be seen as one action of God. This idea has been firmly enunciated by a number of contemporary theologians. Thus Gordon Kaufman writes:

For a monotheistic theology . . . it is *the whole course of history* from its initiation in God's creative activity to its consummation when God ultimately achieves his purposes, that should be conceived as God's act in the primary sense. (Kaufman, *God the Problem*, Cambridge, MA, Harvard University Press, 1972, p. 137)

And John Hick has written in a similar vein:

The most basic and general conception of an action, as we use the word in relation to humanity and as we may apply it analogously in relation to deity, is that of an event enacting an agent's intention. In this basic sense God's continuous creation/salvation of the world is his action. (Michael Goulder and John Hick, *Why Believe in God?*, London, SCM, 1983, p. 73)

. . .

Is there then any other model open to us, which will leave more room for the independence on which I have been insisting? Austin Farrer suggests at one point the model of 'the good novelist who . . . gets a satisfactory story out of the natural behaviour of the characters he conceives'. Dorothy Sayers regarded that as the best available analogy to creation out of nothing. She claims that 'the free-will of a genuinely created character has a certain reality, which the author will deny at his peril'. But she is properly cautious about this claimed independence of characters within the novel. It is certainly something very much less substantial than the independence of real people. The model may be strengthened a little if we move from the idea of a novel to that of an improvised drama, in which the actors are each given the basic character of the person he or she is to represent and the general setting in which their interaction is to be worked out but in which they are left free to determine experimentally how the drama is to develop. In the process of getting deeper into their parts and discovering their reactions to one another in the given situation, they may be led on to enact the kind of drama which the author had always intended and already envisaged in principle though not in detail. The resultant drama would be both the author's and the actors', though we would be more ready to speak of the author as agent of the drama as a whole than as agent of any of the individual speeches or incidents within it.

. . .

'The incarnation is,' in John Macquarrie's phrase, 'the supreme providential act or miracle of history.' And that supremacy has normally been understood to imply not merely that the person of Christ and the events of his life are of central importance for the life of faith but that they are distinct in kind. It has never been easy to spell out precisely the nature of that distinctness. It is tempting, therefore, to see in the reinterpretation of other claimants to be cases of divine intervention or miracle along the lines that I have been suggesting an opportunity for clarifying the distinctness of the incarnation and the resurrection. May not they be seen as unique cases of special divine action, of a kind which in the past has mistakenly been claimed to be the pattern of God's acting on a much wider scale? But such a view has awkward implications . . .

> The isolation of incarnation and resurrection as prime and crucial instances of direct divine action, while it may seem a concession to modernity, effectively falsifies the role they formerly played. Once peaks in a landscape full of hills, all seen as such instances, they now stand out like naked pillars of rock in a plain. (Leslie Houlden, in *Journal of Theological Studies*, XXXIV, 1983, p. 378)

It distances Jesus from the rest of history in the kind of way that led Marcion [*a second century heretic*] to see him as the emissary of some higher God, other than the creator.

For reasons of this sort, theological as opposed to popular reaction to the idea of treating incarnation and resurrection as such radical exceptions to the normal pattern of God's dealing with the world has been generally unfavourable. And this negative reaction is shared by critics and upholders of the traditional doctrines alike. It is perhaps not surprising to find Michael Goulder speaking of 'the implausibility of a theology which allows that the world has been going for four billion years and posits only two actions of God, one 1982 and one 1952 years ago'. But David Brown reacts in a very similar way, if with a diametrically opposed solution to the problem raised. 'Unless,' he writes,

> one is prepared to endorse an interventionist view of God (that over and above his general ordering of the world there are certain specific actions which he performs within our historical, temporal framework), then the very idea of an Incarnation will inevitably seem such a startling exception to the uniform pattern of God's relation to the world as to be, quite literally, incredible. (David Brown, *The Divine Trinity*, London, Duckworth, 1985, p. x)

It is worth noting that his opposition to any understanding of the incarnation as 'a unique exception to the normal pattern of divine activity' is not based simply on its incredibility. He declares a little later on that his principal reason for rejecting such a view is a religious one, namely that it would mean that 'Christ's experience would have no analogy to our own and thus be of no clear relevance to us'.

So the case against treating incarnation and resurrection as divine acts of an altogether unique kind seems to me a very strong one. David Brown's acceptance of that case leads to a strengthening of his conviction that a wholeheartedly interventionist account of God is what we ought to adopt generally. The wide range of theological considerations . . . hold me back from taking that route. The alternative road that I propose to follow is, therefore, to ask whether there are ways in which the convictions traditionally embodied in the doctrines of incarnation and resurrection can be preserved by the opposite move of seeking to bring them within the pattern of understanding God's action that we have developed so far.

Vincent Brümmer, 'Farrer, Wiles and the Causal Joint', *Modern Theology*, 8, 1, 1992, pp. 10–11

There are mainly three ways in which I can know your intentions. First of all, I can know what you intend because you tell me. Secondly, I can infer your intentions from my knowledge of your character. Thus I presume that you are not acting out of character and that your intentions now are the same as I knew them to be when you were acting in similar circumstances in the past. Thirdly, I can infer your intentions from my knowledge of human nature or of the moral standards of the cultural community to which you belong. I presume that your intentions in doing what I perceive you to do are similar to those I know myself and other people (especially those belonging to the same cultural community as you do) to have when they act under similar circumstances. . . .

This analysis of intentional action also applies when we decide whether we are to ascribe an event to God. Even though God's agency is a necessary condition for every event, this does not entail that we should identify every particular event as an act of God. We only ascribe those events to him which he brings about *intentionally* and not those events which are unintended side effects of his intentional acts. In other words, we only ascribe those events to his agency in which he realizes his purposes, and not events which he permits even though they are contrary to his positive will. 'There is much that is contrary to God's positive will. He may permit, but he does not countenance or condone. Angels and men are in open rebellion against him'. This analysis enables us on the one hand to agree with Wiles that 'the whole process of the bringing into being of the world, which is still going on, needs to be seen as one action of God', on condition that we take that to mean that God's agency is a necessary condition for the occurrence of every event that takes place in the world. Contrary to Wiles, we can on the other hand also make sense of the claim that some particular events rather than others may be identified as acts of God, in the sense that we hold God's agency responsible for them and not for the others, even though he could have prevented these others from occurring.

1.3 Indirect divine action and the universal hand of God

Thomas F. Tracy, 'Divine Action', in Philip L. Quinn and Charles Taliaferro (eds), *A Companion to Philosophy of Religion*, Oxford, Blackwell, 1997, pp. 300–1, 303–5

The distinction between general and particular divine providence has often been collapsed in modern theology (e.g. by Schleiermacher), so that particular providence is understood exclusively as the outworking of general providence in specific cases. For example, an event in the natural world (say, a strong east wind as the fleeing Jews approach the sea of reeds) may be the result of the ordinary operations of natural law and yet also be understood to express God's particular purposes for the community whose destiny is especially affected by that event. Indeed, the entire history of the world, to the extent that it flows from causal laws and initial conditions established by God, can be regarded as an extended act of God mediated through natural processes. On this account, events can be identified as 'special divine acts' in so far as they play a distinctive role in revealing and/or advancing divine purposes that were initially written into the program of history. Such a view denies, however, that God acts within historical processes to turn events in a new direction, bringing about developments that would not have occurred but for this particular divine initiative. The elimination of special divine action, in this strong sense, has theologically significant consequences (for example, in Christology and soteriology), and so is a matter of debate in contemporary theology.

These rich patterns of talk about divine action raise a number of compelling philosophical and theological questions. There are, in the first place, puzzles about the coherence of the concept of God as an agent of intentional actions. Are some of the properties that theists have traditionally ascribed to God incompatible with the claim that God acts? Second, questions arise about the relation of God's actions to the operations of created causes in the natural order. This question has especially dominated modern considerations of particular divine action, given the rise of the natural sciences and the 'disenchantment' of nature as a scene of supernatural activity.

A number of the properties that many (but not all) theists have ascribed to God may be thought to be inconsistent with the claim that God is an agent of intentional actions. Consider, for example, the claims that (a) God is incorporeal and is not located in space, and (b) God is not in time but exists in timeless eternity. Can a being that is in neither space nor time coherently be said to act?

. . .

A second set of questions about divine action has to do with the relation of God's activity to the operations of created causes and to the order of nature. It is often said that God acts in and through the processes of nature and history. How might this be understood? What is the relation between traditional theistic affirmations of particular divine action in the world, on the one hand, and scientific descriptions of the world as an intelligible law-governed structure, on the other?

In approaching these questions, it is useful to make a distinction between actions that are direct, or basic, and those that are indirect or mediated. Agents often perform one action (opening a window) by doing another (moving the body in the required ways). An indirect action is brought about by means of action under another description, and any action of this sort must, on pain of infinite regress, originate in an action that the agent undertakes without having to perform any prior intentional action as the means to it. This will be the agent's basic action.

Theists typically have held that God acts both directly and indirectly, choosing in creation to establish and then to act through an order of created causes. God's creative act of calling the world into being is a direct, or basic, action; the divine agent decrees that the world shall be, and it is. So, too, the action of sustaining the world in existence will be direct; if God were no longer to conserve the existence of finite things, they would instantaneously cease to be. Not all of God's actions need be direct, however. God may choose to bestow various causal powers upon created things, and to bring about effects by means of these 'secondary' causes. Rather than producing each finite event directly (e.g. causing water in a kettle to boil spontaneously), God endows created things with causal efficacy of their own, instituting a natural order in which the water is heated by means of a flame. God alone directly and at every moment causes finite things *to be* (that is, to be *ex nihilo* ['*out of nothing*'], rather than merely to undergo change). But God empowers creatures to cause *changes* in other existing things, including the changes that we ordinarily call 'coming into (or passing out of) existence,' as in birth and death. These effects are brought about both by God and by the finite cause, though on different levels (for example, see Aquinas, *Summa Theologiae*, Ia.105.5). God is the primary cause, whose creative action establishes and sustains the network of secondary causes through which the history of the world unfolds. Creatures, in exercising the causal powers God has given them, are the instruments of God's indirect action.

It might be held that this account does not fully convey the depth of creatures' dependence upon God in their operation as secondary causes. According to medieval scholastic theologians, it is not enough that God creates and sustains finite entities and structures their causal powers. Beyond this, God must also act directly with creatures if they are to exercise those powers. This divine concurrence, or cooperation, is a necessary but not sufficient condition for the finite cause to produce its effect. God acts as a general cause, empowering all creatures in their causal operations. Since the divine concurrence is universal and uniform, the difference in the effect from case to case reflects the specific nature of the creaturely cause. Without this direct divine cooperation, it was claimed, creatures will simply fail to produce effects at all. The idea of divine concurrence has received relatively little attention in modern discussions of divine action, in part because it is unclear what concurrence amounts to and why it is needed over and above the affirmation that God creates and sustains a world in which creatures possess and exercise causal powers.

These basic affirmations about God's direct and indirect agency make possible an account of particular, or special, divine action in the world. Note, in the first place, that if the causal history of the world is strictly deterministic, then every event within it can be regarded as an indirect act of God mediated through the operation of secondary causes. God can realize particular divine purposes simply by designing the causal laws and initial conditions of the natural order so as to guarantee that the intended result will be achieved. If one holds that all of God's actions in the world take this form, then the result (as we noted above) is to absorb particular providence entirely into God's general providence in creation and conservation.

Traditionally, however, theists have affirmed that God also acts directly within the world to serve particular purposes not built into history at the beginning. In a deterministic universe, such actions must constitute miraculous departures from the ordinary course of nature; this will be the case whether these divine interventions are overtly spectacular 'mighty acts' or exquisitely subtle contributions to the mental or spiritual lives of human agents. For this reason, a succession of modern theologians have held that we can no longer affirm direct and particular divine action in history. They have been led to this view, at least in part, by their belief that universal causal determinism either has been established by the natural sciences or is presupposed by scientific methods of inquiry. There are good reasons, however, to deny both these claims about the sciences; indeed, there currently are compelling scientific grounds (for example, in the dominant interpretation of quantum mechanics) for thinking that universal determinism is false.

In a non-deterministic universe, the simple picture of God's indirect action through the causal structures of nature is complicated by the fact that at least some of these causal chains will be incomplete. Events will lack causally sufficient antecedent conditions in the natural order when there is an element of indeterministic chance in their history and/or when they result from human actions that are free in the strong (i.e. 'libertarian') sense. God could choose to determine events of either sort; they would then be chance or (more controversially) free only in their relation to other finite events. When God does not do this, however, these undetermined events may initiate causal chains in the world which cannot simply be attributed to God as (indirect) divine acts, though God directly gives them their being and permits them to play this role in history.

Note that the integration of chance into the order of nature provides a structure within which God's particular providential actions need not involve any miraculous suspension of natural law. In selectively determining events that occur by chance on the finite level, God does not displace natural causes that would otherwise have determined that event, and God's activity could be entirely compatible with whatever the sciences may tell us about the distribution of such events in regular probabilistic patterns. In this way, the world God has made could display both a reliable causal structure and an inherent openness to novelty, allowing for a seamless integration of natural law and ongoing direct involvement by God in shaping the course of events.

Theists, then, may affirm both that God acts universally in the creation and conservation of all things and that God acts in particular events in history. The latter may be understood in several ways: (1) as indirect action through secondary causal chains that extend from God's direct actions; (2) as direct action that brings about events outside the regularities of nature; and (3) as direct action that determines natural indeterminacies within the regular structures of nature. In any or all of these ways, God can affect the course of history and interact with human beings to achieve particular divine purposes.

Vernon White, *The Fall of a Sparrow: A Concept of Special Divine Action*, Exeter, Paternoster, 1985, pp. 115–17

Austin Farrer compares the way a good author constructs his work to God's universal action. . . . 'While [God] thinks out the orderly life of a man's mind, he must at the same time think out the action of the minute physical underlyings which carry the work of his brain' (Farrer, *A Science of God*, p. 78). With such universal scope of action God thus can and does embrace the whole of our environment. It is directly implied by the doctrine of God as creator and Lord of creation, and calls to mind Karl Barth's ringing insistence:

> . . . [God's] will is accomplished directly and His decisions are made and fulfilled in all creaturely occurrence both great and small. He would not be God at all if He were not the living God, if there were a single point where He was absent or inactive, or only partly active, or restricted in His action. (Barth, *Church Dogmatics*, III, 1, ET Edinburgh, T & T Clark, p. 133)

This universal scope of action could have far-reaching implications for the efficacy of action (though Farrer himself does not seem anxious to press this point as far as we shall be doing). For example, using Farrer's language, if I could 'think out' the condition of my wife's total situation, and furthermore, if I have equally 'thought out' the condition of every conceivable situation which might be locked into hers, or which might be locked into hers by any action she undertakes, is there not a sense in which I could by my actions so 'load the dice' that whatever she does (though still as a free agent, acting from within herself and with her own intention) can nonetheless be woven into the fabric of the past, present and future to carry my meaning and purpose? It could be something as simple as ensuring she met the kind of person to persuade her in a particular course of action: for with unlimited scope of action in other people's situations as well as her own I could guarantee this without risk or uncertainty (which would be seen to belong to our finitude rather than to the notion of interacting free personal agency itself).

But what would this mean for her freedom, or the freedom of any agent? To what extent does this imply an unacceptable manipulation? Here an important distinction must be made, for there are two distinct ways of construing the business of 'loading the dice'. It could mean so arranging and ordering reality that a creature has to act (and, also, to intend) in a certain way; so constituting his nature and the nature of circumstances surrounding him that he intends what you want him to intend: his act is your act, in a one-to-one correspondence. *Or*, it could mean so arranging and ordering reality that whatever intention the creature has, and indeed enacts in his particular context, carries your intention in a wider context of meaning. In short, so acting that his real act is a sub-act within your master-act (to go back to Kaufman's terminology), but you are playing a different drama. Thus we can return to Judas and insist again that if it is in him to betray Jesus, so be it, but it will carry a meaning within God's intention other than Judas' intentions: Judas' act will be a sub-act in God's overall purpose. It is of course the latter of these two alternative senses of 'loading the dice' which is being canvassed here in support of the paradox of double agency. The former seriously compromises the sense in which the secondary agent remains free agent, yet of the latter it can still be said that whatever the agent freely does is encompassed without risk in the primary agent's action.

To further support this picture, another objection must also be dealt with. It may be argued with some justice that it is very hard to see how that reality which is to be ordered around an individual (so that the divine intention will in any eventuality be fulfilled) is sufficiently pliable to the divine hand for the overall conception to be sustained. After all, the context to be arranged is constituted both by other natural activity systems proceeding under a general pattern of uniformity (or indeed with a measure of indeterminacy at some levels), and free decisions of other human agents. Both kinds of activity are to be respected. And even to *know* what every 'necessary' and contingent interlocking event will be is not yet equivalent to arranging those events. Most difficult of all, to the extent that the reality which is to be 'arranged' around the individual and his free decisions is constituted by other contingencies (whether of human or 'natural' activity) it may be argued that there is insufficient stability, no purchase for the divine hand to weave the necessary pattern, only an infinite regress of creaturely contingencies.

In fact this kind of objection reflects an inadequate grasp of what is meant by the universal scope of the divine action. When it is being claimed that God 'thinks out' every activity and its interaction with other activities, this is not simply a statement about what God knows; rather, we have to conceive of every sequence of activity arranged 'from the beginning' according to its 'future' interaction with other activities. 'From the beginning' does not here imply that all effects are present in the first single cause of the world, but rather that the world is a continuously woven mesh of newly emerging activity sequences, and at every point of inception (and continuance) God's creative intention is exercising its hidden causal efficacy. That the world is such a mesh of newly emerging activity sequences is most visible from the human perspective by analogy with human action at the juncture of 'history' and 'nature'; human intention changes the course of natural sequences, whether it is the building of a dam or the binding up of a wound. From the divine perspective we have to conceive of *every* sequence begun and continued with God's creative will, developing by interaction with other created sequences so that it develops both in accordance with its own nature and the divine intention which knows what each interaction will in fact produce. In the case of knowing subjects the divine will may indeed be known (in experience and revelation) to be presenting itself persuasively (but not coercively), and so be specifically known to affect some sequences; but that human knowledge is secondary to the prior divine knowledge as to whether in fact the human agent will respond – and if there is no response all other relevant interlocking sequences will have accommodated this fact 'from the beginning'.

1.4 Human freedom and divine frustration

William Alston, 'How to Think about Divine Action', in Brian
Hebblethwaite and Edward Henderson (eds), *Divine Action*,
Edinburgh, T & T Clark, 1990, pp. 57–9

[W]e 'post-mythological' moderns are not constrained by anything we are
justified in believing about the causal order to deny that God acts in the
world outside that order. There may be theological reasons for declining
to think of divine activity in this way, but here I am only concerned to
argue that our general knowledge leaves the possibility open. However I
am by no means suggesting that God can act in the world *only* by acting
outside the natural order. On the contrary, I wish to affirm that God
can, and does, act in and through the action of natural causes. . . .
[Here] the analogy of the artisan and his tool seems to me quite appropriate. When I split a log with an axe, it is true both that the axe splits
the log and that I split the log. Similarly if God creates, orders, and con-
serves the natural order to carry out his purposes, then it is true both
[that] the bee pollinates the flower and that God does so. Let me now
briefly comment on a few problems that come up for this mode of divine
action.

Many of those who argue that God is an agent of all creaturely
happenings take God to will every detail of the world process, including
putatively free choices and doings of human beings. This makes possible
a satisfyingly simple picture. God institutes the natural order, realising in
advance all the details of its working out, and instituting it in order to bring
about all those details. Every natural event, except for the first one if
any, is brought about by other natural events that are used by God as
instruments for that purpose. But if human free choices and actions are
not willed by God (God endows these creatures with the capacity to
decide such matters themselves and allows them to do so), they constitute a rent in this simple picture. God didn't institute the natural
order to bring these events about; they are not (wholly) brought about
by natural causes. We might try to handle this difficulty just by making
an exception: God is the agent of all and only those natural events that
he has willed to happen just as they do. But the trouble goes deeper.
Human free actions themselves have consequences. Hence any natural
happenings in the causal ancestry of which there is some creaturely free
choice are not such as to be planned by God just on the basis of the
kind of natural causal order he set up. Thus the biological and ecological
processes involved in areas under human cultivation could not have

been planned by God just on the basis of his knowledge of what would result from the beings he created and the laws of nature he ordained. Of course, if he has foreknowledge of human free actions he can take account of those in further planning. But, on the present hypothesis of human free will, he cannot complete his planning for the uses of created instruments prior to any creative decisions. For the fore-knowledge of human free choices will be prior knowledge of what those beings actually choose in situations in which they actually find them-selves. And they don't find themselves in one set of circumstances rather than another, indeed they do not even exist, until God makes some decisions to create. Thus it would seem that in order to accom-modate human free will we are forced into thinking of God of making a number of separate *ad hoc* decisions (as to how to react to free choices of creatures) after the initial institution of the natural order. We have lost the beautiful simplicity of a scheme in which, just by an initial act of creation, God thereby becomes the primary agent of every natural happening. We can, however, recapture that simplicity if we can attribute to God what the sixteenth century Jesuit theologian, Luis de Molina, called 'middle knowledge'. This is knowledge not of what actually existing creatures freely choose in actual situations, but of what various possible free creatures *would* choose in various possible situations. Armed with such knowledge God could create a total order in which everything, both naturally determined happenings and creaturely free choices, would interact to bring about just the results he is aiming at.

David Brown, 'God and Symbolic Action', in Brian Hebblethwaite and Edward Henderson (eds), *Divine Action,* **Edinburgh, T & T Clark, 1990, pp. 104–7**

To speak of an unembodied agent like God 'acting' does not seem to me to present any insuperable difficulties. Not only do phenomena like telepathy and telekinesis give ready intelligibility to the idea of acting without a physical medium, even in the ordinary human case where such a medium seems essential, this apparent essentiality surely stems merely from the contingent fact of constant concurrence and not because the action would be unintelligible without it. Further confirmation of this emerges from the realisation that what makes something an action is its intentionality, and we can know our intentions without first checking our bodily behaviour. In other words, because what is indispensable to the concept of action is intentionality and not a particular medium, there can be no logical incoherence in the notion of action, including divine action, that involves no such medium.

But why place such action within an interventionist framework? 'Interventionist' is perhaps not entirely a happy term. It has two principal defects. First, it suggests that God is uninvolved with the world except where he is specifically intervening. Secondly, intervention can very easily suggest manipulation or authoritarian interference. My stress . . . on a free human response demonstrates clearly that the latter idea of manipulation is very far from my mind. 'Interactionist' might be a better description. But there is some truth in the first charge. For, while I wish to insist on God's creative role as sustainer and orderer of the universe, I do find it hard to locate sufficient involvement in the non-interventionist cases, such that the accusation can then be resisted that the term 'action' is here not merely being used in an attenuated sense. Thus it is only action in the same way as troops winning a battle can be described as the action of the general leading them, or the bursting of a dam as the incompetent action of the engineer who built it. Clearly in these two situations the size of possible contribution from the general and engineer can range from the merely permissive, for example a doddery, senile general giving a command to brave troops, to the absolutely decisive, the engineer building a dam unable to restrain even ordinary levels of water. So, in answer to what Owen Thomas in *God's Activity in the World* has called the 'fundamental' question, 'Does God act in all events or only in some?', it is clear that we must say that there are degrees of appropriateness in speaking of divine action, but that these culminate in what I, for better or worse, have labelled the interventionist cases.

There seems to me at least two good reasons why the term 'divine action' must find its most natural application in this context. Both are linked in the sense that they are drawing out implications of the fact that 'action' belongs to the category of the 'personal'. For, as we have seen, integral to the notion are intentions and only persons can have intentions.

First, in ascribing intervention to God we are only in effect according to him the same kind of personal freedom of interaction that we would wish to ascribe to ourselves. For many, Christians and non-Christians alike, would agree that we have a contra-causal freedom that can be subsumed under no laws, whether psychological, physiological or otherwise, and that is precisely in the exercise of that freedom that we most show ourselves to be persons and not automata. Why then should divine activity be brought under any such laws? The failure of theologians to take with sufficient seriousness this analogy with our human situation is well illustrated by F. B. Dilley's article, 'Does the "God who acts" really act?' (in Thomas, *op. cit.*, pp. 45–60). He ends by presenting us with a stark choice between miracles and uniform natural laws, with the former discounted because of the difficulty of believing in them in the modern age. Thomas rightly points out that this is not as difficult as is often supposed, but, more importantly for our purposes here, it needs to be observed that he has totally ignored a third alternative. For, just as our interaction with each other can be subsumed under no natural law, so also with God's gracious interaction upon us. In short, so far from intervention necessarily involving the miraculous, it seems indispensable if we are to allow God the same power and dignity of action as we are prepared to ascribe to ourselves.

Secondly, in insisting that not all divine action is of the same kind we are doing something also to preserve our own personal freedom and dignity, as it has been given to us by God. For were we to say that it is all of the same sustaining kind subsumable under natural laws, at once both the divine distance and the divine closeness would be swallowed up in one, except perhaps subjectively, whereas both are in fact integral if human action and its relation to the divine are properly to be described as personal. Thus one needs divine distance in order to preserve room for independent human decision-making, and a non-ubiquitous divine closeness or activity if the relation is to be regarded as personal, that is, with intentions shaped in response to the free actions of the other. It is precisely because of uncertainty whether Farrer's theory of 'double agency' meets this criterion that I find it so unsatisfactory, or at any rate the version of it . . . defended by Vernon White in *The Fall of the Sparrow*. He develops the idea with an impressive consistency and clarity, but that in turn makes it all the more easy to see what is wrong with the idea, at least as he presents it. What White is most concerned to defend is the divine sovereignty, that nothing can be allowed to frustrate the divine intention. So significantly Barth is quoted to the effect that God 'would not be God . . . if there were a *single* point where he was . . . only *partly* active or restricted in his action' (my italics), and accordingly natural events and human actions are both equally brought under the rubric that 'whatever happens is caught up to serve God's intention'. But it seems to me that to insist that in any situation God is always an agent, always more than just a permitting cause, even when due qualification is made for the problem of evil, cannot but be to call into question human freedom. If we are truly in the divine image and thus truly persons, this cannot but mean an ability to frustrate the divine purpose, and frustrate it ultimately. For to suggest otherwise must inevitably mean envisaging

God interfering in human freedom to ensure that his purposes are always realized.

1.5 Images of divine control

Doctrine Commission of the General Synod of the Church of England, *We Believe in God: A Report by the Doctrine Commission of the General Synod of the Church of England,* **London, Church House Publishing, 1987, pp. 148–54, 156**

Many Christians would hold that the authentic and authoritative model of divine control is given to us in the biblical image of the Sovereignty or Kingship of God. Certainly this image pervades the Bible. But its force may be lost on the modern enquirer simply because the power of kings is so much diminished and their role so greatly changed in the modern world. What we expect of kings is not what the biblical writers expected. In us their image evokes respect but may inspire little awe. Furthermore the biblical expectation, though greater than our own, is not entirely consistent or homogeneous. Two rather different images of kingship, two rather different 'pictures' of what a good king is and does, appear in the Bible.

One such image appears in the Wisdom of Solomon, and is quite close to Plato's image or concept of the 'philosopher-king'. Here kingship is 'the upholding of the people' (6:24). The king will 'set the people in order' (8:14) and 'order the world according to equity and righteousness' (9:3). He knows 'all things that are either secret or manifest' (7:21). The wisdom which teaches him what is right also enables him to achieve it in his kingdom – for that wisdom is 'the worker of all things', 'cannot be obstructed', 'oversees all things' (7:22–3) and, 'reaching from one end to the other, sweetly orders all things' (8:1). The image is of someone by whose wisdom and power everything is so controlled that nothing can be present in the kingdom which is alien to his will, nothing can happen in it save by his 'ordering'.

In Psalm 72 a distinctly different image of kingship appears, which may be called the image of the 'saviour-king'. In the realm of the saviour-king certain things appear which are quite definitely not in accordance with the royal will; and the greatness of the king lies in the readiness and effectiveness with which he redeems or redresses these things. The king will 'defend the poor . . . defend the children of the poor and punish the wrong-doer' (verses 2 and 4). He will 'deliver the poor when he crieth; the needy also and him that hath no helper' (verse 12), and in his sight the blood of the poor will be 'dear' (verse 14). Clearly it is not by the will of the king that poverty and oppression exist in his kingdom. His role as a good king is to respond to them with remedy and redress, to act as King David is prepared to act when Nathan tells him of the poor man deprived of his 'one ewe lamb' [2 *Samuel 12:5–6*]. Unlike the philosopher-king, in whose kingdom nothing can occur which is alien to the royal will, the saviour-king is constantly meeting, redressing and redeeming that which is alien to his will.

So the biblical image of kingship has at least two facets, and both these facets appear when human kingship is used as a model of divine sovereignty. Sometimes biblical writers insist that a certain event, disastrous as it appeared to human eyes, was in fact willed by God for his own purposes. So it was that Pharaoh's heart was hardened and that Nineveh repented when Jonah preached. In these cases God is represented, so to speak, as the philosopher-king in whose realm, despite all appearances, everything happens precisely as he wills and ordains it. But in many other cases it is as the saviour-king that God appears – responding to actions and situations which are alien to his will, hearing and punishing when the blood of Abel cries to him from the ground, turning to good the evil which Joseph's brothers do to him, avenging the death of Uriah the Hittite by the death of Bathsheba's child, punishing the sin of his people or remitting punishment in response to Moses' intercession, pleading with his people through the prophets, stirred to action when they are enslaved in Egypt or oppressed by foreign invaders. In such situations it is very clear that God is responding to what he has not willed, that he is the saviour-king, acting to set right what is wrong, to redress, redeem and deliver.

In the kingdom of the philosopher-king all is, so to speak, 'programmed' by and in conformity with the sovereign's will. In the kingdom of the saviour-king many things must be won into conformity with the sovereign's will. Both these images of divine control are present in the Bible, but it is undoubtedly the second which predominates; and this image, in contrast to that of the philosopher-king, suggests a God who is not only attentive to his people but also close to them, involved with them. The philosopher-king is raised above any involvement in such distresses as his people may experience, because those distresses are actually willed by him for his own good purposes. But the saviour-king is so close to his people that he can be roused to anger by the appearance among them of things alien to his will, and be vulnerable to the grief which cries, 'What have I done to you, O my people, and wherein have I wearied you?' God the saviour-king shepherds his people, leads them, pioneers the way for them out of slavery and the shadow of death. He is acquainted with his people's distresses from the inside. He bears their griefs and carries their sorrows; he shares what his people endure. He travels with his people through the wilderness – even 'dwelling in tents' as they do – and, as their leader, is not exempt from the perseverance and faithfulness which that journey must entail. The important biblical concept of the faithfulness of God suggests very powerfully his involvement in the labours and struggles of his people.

It has already been remarked that kingship in the modern world is not what it was: a modern king dignifies rather than controls the nation's life. Therefore it will not be much help to a modern enquirer if we explain our understanding of God's control of the world in terms of the model of the saviour-king. Can this model be translated or updated? One possible and promising translation is into the language of artistic creation, an activity much analysed and discussed today.

The artist in any field gives being to a work of art. It is he or she who makes it what it is. Admittedly, pre-existent materials are used; but of the work of art as such the artist alone is the creator – it is out of the artist's spontaneity that the work of art comes into being. But that spontaneity must be expressed within some kind of form – a canvas of a particular size, a certain verse convention. The artist chooses the form; but the form once chosen exercises a degree of constraint or discipline on his or her spontaneity. Spontaneity does not simply flow, nor is art simply 'doodling' with a pencil or strumming as one pleases upon a stringed instrument. In artistic creativity a certain struggle or adventure is involved – the endeavour to contain and express spontaneity within form. In this endeavour there is no programme or blueprint to follow. The artist is reaching out towards a vision or possibility which is not yet fully formulated even in the 'inward eye', and which appears with increasing clarity only as the work proceeds.

If we now apply this model to God, we may find that it helps us to approach some aspects of the age-old problem of evil. Having freely chosen to create something in a particular 'medium', God may no longer be free to escape the constraints which that medium imposes. The question why God 'allows' an earthquake, a volcanic eruption, a flood or a drought – things which may take a heavy toll of innocent human life – needs to be set in the context of the fact that the creation of any environment suitable for living beings (which in any case depends upon an extraordinarily fine balance in the chemistry of the atmosphere) entails accepting a variable climate with all those instabilities which lead (from a human point of view) to disasters.

There is, however, a further aspect of the artist model which may take us somewhat nearer to the heart of evil and suffering. At this point it may be helpful to think of a sculptor rather than a painter. Once the medium (a block of stone or wood) is chosen, then, as we have said, it imposes its own constraints. In the artist's mind is a clear idea of the intended shape; but certain unforeseen factors may intervene. The material used may have a grain, a knot or an imperfection which resists the creative intention; or a cut may be made which is actually 'wrong', in the sense of not being exactly what was intended. It is here that the greatness of the artist appears in the skill and patience needed to 'win back' that which is 'wrong'. The wrong is not simply left as it is, as it might be by an inferior artist, nor is it simply eliminated or cast aside – for it is an authentic element in the artist's spontaneity. Still less, of course, is the whole work abandoned. . . . It is the exercise of a special and unique kind of 'control' – a control which redeems rather than prevents the wrong, which draws into the overall purpose that which obstructs that purpose. The control of the artist is a 'saving' rather than a 'programming' form of control. 'Creation' is also a continuing 'redemption.'

[A]rtistic creativity . . . is not strictly a biblical model, but there are strong and clear resonances between what it suggests and what is suggested by the dominant biblical image of God as saviour-king. The model suggests that, while the world and everything which it contains is God's work, some of the things and events within the world are 'not what God wants' and are in need of winning back or redeeming into the ambit of his good purpose. To some people this will be a feature of the model which enhances its credibility. It will also be more credible to some, because it suggests a God who, so far from presiding in distant serenity over a fallen and anguished world, is constantly involved in the close encounter of redemption.

The artist-model is not, of course, of use only to throw light on the problem of evil. It is also a way of picturing the creation itself. In this respect it is certainly more adequate than the 'clockmaker' model, which has been popular ever since the eighteenth century, and which still affects the thinking of many religious people today. According to this model, the Creator is imagined as setting up an immensely complex piece of machinery and then letting it run according to its own laws and mechanisms. Everything that happens is the result of something that happened previously, and this long interconnected series of happenings can in theory be traced back to the original devising of the Creator. It was a model which was always felt to be seriously inadequate as soon as human beings were brought into the picture, because it presupposed that the Creator had planned to its last detail the great history of life on this earth, and that, having set it in motion, he was now allowing it to run its predetermined course. Such total determinism, even apart from the philosophical difficulties it raises, has never been felt to be compatible with the experience of what it is to be a free human being; and even as a way of understanding the world of nature, the 'clockmaker' model is quite out of touch with contemporary science. Modern genetic and evolutionary theory cannot possibly be reconciled with such a crudely mechanistic interpretation of the universe.

But the artist-model in turn becomes less appropriate as soon as it becomes necessary to offer an interpretation of the phenomenon of human life. Even if the materials an artist uses bring with them some constraints, it is still the artist who is in control. The materials are inanimate.

. . .

To complete our account of the relationship between the creator and his creation – or between God and human beings – we must therefore explore a further 'model'. The one that lies to hand is one which occurs in many religions and is of great importance in both Judaism and Christianity. This is the model of parent and child. The parents are (in a sense) the 'creator' of their child; but the child is endowed with its own independence, its own free will, and the relationship of the parents to the child may become the arena for a prolonged tussle of wills. Parents consider they know what is best for the child, and seek to direct it in the right paths. The child believes it knows better, and may disregard or disobey the admonitions of its parents. In the early stages the parents may have to use force or material sanctions to impose their will on the child. But as the child grows into adulthood it becomes physically independent of them. They experience the joy and the risk of letting the child be itself, though they may also from time to time use persuasion, accompanied perhaps by threats of disinheritance or other material disadvantages, to influence the child's free and adult decisions.

. . .

[S]urely we can press the analogy and say that the father suffers from the disobedience of his children, that the creator, by loving his creation, makes himself vulnerable to being spurned and abused by them?

Topics for discussion

1 Is divine action best conceived as a single act? Does this mean necessarily conceiving of God in deistic, that is non-interventionist terms? What implications might this have for other Christian doctrines?

2 How does the question of divine action relate to the doctrine of providence? Is a doctrine of providence possible on Wiles' account? Is the interventionist view necessarily committed to the belief that God always gets his way in the end (cf. Barth, White)? Or is providence a doctrine about divine care, rather than particular results?

3 Can a distinction between general and special providence be justified?

4 Does speaking of God as intervening in, or interacting with, the world necessarily lead us to think of miracle? If not, what is the difference?

5 What do you make of the claim that in any given event there are two agents, the human and the divine (called 'double agency' by Austin Farrer)? Is it important to speak of God being more of an agent in some events than others? Should one distinguish degrees of divine involvement (for example, in a divine sustaining role as creator; grace as giving an added push to human action; miracles with God as sole agent)?

6 Are there any significant analogies with human action which might help us to make sense of divine action?

2 Miracles

2.1 Miracle in the Bible

Genesis 18:1–3; 9–14

18 ¹The LORD appeared to Abraham by the oaks of Mamre, as he sat at the entrance of his tent in the heat of the day. ²He looked up and saw three men standing near him. When he saw them, he ran from the tent entrance to meet them, and bowed down to the ground. ³He said, 'My lord, if I find favour with you, do not pass by your servant. . . . ⁹They said to him, 'Where is your wife Sarah?' And he said, 'There, in the tent.' ¹⁰Then one said, 'I will surely return to you in due season, and your wife Sarah shall have a son.' And Sarah was listening at the tent entrance behind him. ¹¹Now Abraham and Sarah were old, advanced in age; it had ceased to be with Sarah after the manner of women. ¹²So Sarah laughed to herself, saying, 'After I have grown old, and my husband is old, shall I have pleasure?' ¹³The LORD said to Abraham, 'Why did Sarah laugh, and say, "Shall I indeed bear a child, now that I am old?" ¹⁴Is anything too wonderful for the LORD? At the set time I will return to you, in due season, and Sarah shall have a son.'

Mark 1:40–44a

1 ⁴⁰A leper came to him begging him, and kneeling he said to him, 'If you choose, you can make me clean.' ⁴¹Moved with pity, Jesus stretched out his hand and touched him, and said to him, 'I do choose. Be made clean!' ⁴²Immediately the leprosy left him, and he was made clean. ⁴³After sternly warning him he sent him away at once, ⁴⁴saying to him, 'See that you say nothing to anyone . . .

John 2:1–11

2 On the third day there was a wedding in Cana of Galilee, and the mother of Jesus was there. [2]Jesus and his disciples had also been invited to the wedding. [3]When the wine gave out, the mother of Jesus said to him, 'They have no wine.' [4]And Jesus said to her, 'Woman, what concern is that to you and to me? My hour has not yet come.' [5]His mother said to the servants, 'Do whatever he tells you.' [6]Now standing there were six stone water-jars for the Jewish rites of purification, each holding twenty or thirty gallons. [7]Jesus said to them, 'Fill the jars with water.' And they filled them up to the brim. [8]He said to them, 'Now draw some out, and take it to the chief steward.' So they took it. [9]When the steward tasted the water that had become wine, and did not know where it came from (though the servants who had drawn the water knew), the steward called the bridegroom [10]and said to him, 'Everyone serves the good wine first, and then the inferior wine after the guests have become drunk. But you have kept the good wine until now.' [11]Jesus did this, the first of his signs, in Cana of Galilee, and revealed his glory; and his disciples believed in him.

2.2 Defining miracle

H. H. Farmer, *The World and God: A Study of Prayer, Providence and Miracle in Christian Experience,* **London, Collins, 1963, pp. 103–7**

The fatal mistake is to begin the consideration of miracle from the angle of a scientific or philosophic concept of natural law. Miracle being fundamentally a religious category and not a scientific or philosophic one, the proper place to begin is within the sphere of living religion itself. To define miracle *in limine* ['*on the edge*'], for example, as an event involving suspension of natural laws is to begin in the wrong place. We must first ask what is the significance of miracle for religion; we must define and evaluate it, seek to understand the indispensability of it, within that context and universe of discourse. Thereafter we may go on to enquire how the religious thought of miracle may best be related to those other aspects of the world presented to us through other than specifically religious channels. This does not mean that we wish to isolate our religious judgements from anything that is comprised within our experience as modern people, least of all from the discoveries of science when these are well attested. But the final judgement on a religious matter must be a religious judgement; that is to say, it must be one such as the deeply religious man cannot help making and acting on when he is most livingly aware that God is dealing with him and he with God, as, for example, when in a critical situation he is on his knees at prayer.

To begin, as so many do, by defining a miraculous event in terms of its relation to the system of nature, instead of in terms of its relation to the religious life, affords another example of the dangerous facility with which the abstractions of rational thought can be substituted for, and obscure, the realities of living religious experience. Whatever the word miracle signifies religiously it certainly indicates something which evokes a profound feeling response akin to wonder and awe, as the etymology of the word shows. Yet the definition of miracle as an event involving the suspension of law by omnipotent might leaves this entirely out of account. Nay more, it definitely runs counter to it, and makes it seem out of place. For the possibility of miracle so defined becomes merely part of the rational meaning of omnipotence, and in itself it no more evokes wonder to contemplate omnipotence suspending laws than it does to contemplate impotence submitting to them. The *mirabile* ['*wonder-evoking*'] in the *miraculum* must therefore have another source than the mere thought of the suspension of law by God, and what that source is can be understood only by approaching the whole question from a different angle, from the angle of the religious life itself.

Starting, then, from this angle, the first thing to be said is clear enough, namely, that a miraculous event always enters the religious man's experience as a *revelation* of God . . . Whatever else it may be, it is an event or complex of events through which a man becomes aware of God as active towards himself in and through his own personal situation. It is God acting relevantly to a man's individual situation and destiny; speaking through events because He is active in events; confronting the soul as personal will and purpose in that immediacy of relationship which is nevertheless mediated through the environing world. Unless an event has this quality in some degree to someone it is not, in the religious sense of the term, a miracle.

Paul Tillich, *Systematic Theology*, Vol I, London, Nisbet, 1968, pp. 128–30

The word 'miracle', according to the ordinary definition, designates a happening that contradicts the laws of nature. This definition and the innumerable unverified miracle stories in all religions have rendered the term misleading and dangerous for theological use. But a word which expresses a genuine experience can only be dropped if a substitute is at hand, and it does not seem that such a substitute has been found. The New Testament often uses the Greek word *sēmeion*, 'sign,' pointing to the religious meaning of the miracles. But the word 'sign' without a qualifying addition cannot express this religious meaning. It would be more accurate to add the word 'event' to 'sign' and to speak of *sign-events*. The original meaning of miracle, 'that which produces astonishment,' is quite adequate for describing the 'giving side' of a revelatory experience. But this connotation has been swallowed by the bad connotation of a supranatural interference which destroys the natural structure of events. The bad connotation is avoided in the word 'sign' and the phrase 'sign event.'

While the original naïve religious consciousness accepts astounding stories in connection with divine manifestations without elaborating a supranaturalistic theory of miracles, rationalistic periods make the negation of natural laws the main point in miracle stories. A kind of irrationalist rationalism develops in which the degree of absurdity in a miracle story becomes the measure of its religious value. The more impossible, the more revelatory! Already in the New Testament one can observe that, the later the tradition, the more the anti-natural element is emphasised over against the sign element. In the post-apostolic period, when the apocryphal Gospels were produced, there were no checks against absurdity. Pagans and Christians alike were not so much interested in the presence of the divine in shaking and sign-giving events as they were in the sensation produced in their rationalistic minds by anti-rational happenings. This rationalistic anti-rationalism infected later Christianity, and it is still a burden for the life of the church and for theology.

The manifestation of the mystery of being does not destroy the structure of being in which it becomes manifest. The ecstasy in which the mystery is received does not destroy the rational structure of the mind by which it is received. The sign-event which gives the mystery of revelation does not destroy the rational structure of the reality in which it appears. If these criteria are applied, a meaningful doctrine of sign-events or miracles can be stated.

One should not use the word 'miracle' for events which create astonishment for a certain time, such as scientific discoveries, technical creations, impressive works of art or politics, personal achievements, etc. These cease to produce astonishment after one has become accustomed to them, although a profound admiration of them may remain and even increase. . . . There is an element of astonishment in admiration, but it is not a numinous astonishment; it does not point to a miracle.

. . .

Miracles cannot be interpreted in terms of a supranatural interference in natural processes. If such an interpretation were true, the manifestation of the ground of being would destroy the structure of being; God would be split within himself, as religious dualism has asserted. It would be more adequate to call such a miracle 'demonic,' not because it is produced by 'demons,' but because it discloses a 'structure of destruction'.

. . .

The sign-events in which the mystery of being gives itself consist in special constellations of elements of reality in correlation with special constellations of elements of the mind. A genuine miracle is first of all an event which is astonishing, unusual, shaking, without contradicting the rational structure of reality. In the second place, it is an event which points to the mystery of being, expressing its relation to us in a definite way. In the third place, it is an occurrence which is received as a sign-event in an ecstatic experience. Only if these three conditions are fulfilled can one speak of a genuine miracle. That which does not shake one by its astonishing character has no revelatory power. That which shakes one without pointing to the mystery of being is not miracle but sorcery. That which is not received in ecstasy is a report about the belief in a miracle, not an actual miracle. This is emphasised in the synoptic records of the miracles of Jesus. Miracles are given only to those for whom they are sign-events, to those who receive them in faith. Jesus refuses to perform 'objective' miracles. They are a contradiction in terms. This strict correlation makes it possible to exchange the words describing miracles and those describing ecstasy. One can say that ecstasy is the miracle of the mind and that miracle is the ecstasy of reality.

Keith Ward, *Divine Action*, London, Collins, 1990, pp. 179–81

The sceptical eighteenth century philosopher David Hume performed a great disservice to religion (as he intended to) when he defined a miracle as 'a transgression of a law of nature by a particular volition of the Deity, or by the interposition of some invisible agent'. He thereby presents us with the picture of a clockwork universe, a closed physical system working in a wholly deterministic and regular way. God can only act in such a system by breaking some of its laws and interfering with it. And the implication is that such interferences are quite irrational, or occur in an arbitrary fashion, in accordance simply with the whim of some extra-clockwork being. Or, equally absurdly, they are needed to correct some defect that has developed in the machinery. It was largely because of such a conception that the eighteenth century deists argued that miracles were absurd and unnecessary for a perfect creator, capable of designing non-defective clocks.

It is a great pity that Hume's definition has become widely accepted, for it is misleading in almost every respect. Physicists know that the universe is not clockwork; but more importantly, for a theist the physical universe is not a closed system. Having its origin in God, it is always orientated towards God, finding its true fulfilment in relation to him. Moreover, the universe does not act only in regular, repetitive ways. It contains unique events and processes, emergent states and surprising sequences of probabilistic causal interconnections. The universe stands to God more as a body does to its controlling self than as a machine stands to its maker – though one must be careful not to let this analogy blur the distinctness and freedom of finite persons. God is present throughout the universe, as the overall purposing field which guides its development and shapes particular sequences towards realizing that general purpose in new, imaginative and particular ways. One might better think of God as the purposive causal basis of the universe itself than as the watchmaker tinkering with his artefacts.

With this rather different picture, God's acts need not be seen as interferences with a regular mechanism. They will be expressed in the purposive direction of the physical processes themselves. They will not be arbitrary – God deciding to interfere here but not there – for God will be involved in every part of the structure, as its purposive ground. A miracle will be an extraordinary event, improbable in terms of the physical system considered in itself, but fairly probable in the wider context of a spiritual purpose for the whole system. For it is probable that a created universe will exhibit particular processes which establish or develop a conscious relation to the supernatural basis of the physical system. In such processes, the physical will not be contradicted; it will be perfected beyond its normal temporal state by becoming transparent to the eternal. What is beyond the powers of nature, considered in itself, becomes a natural endowment of creatures which are infused with Divine wisdom and power, and which thereby become vehicles of infinite Spirit and foreshadowings of the divinely willed fulfilment of all things.

Miracles are not just anomalous events which interrupt the seamless processes of nature. They are events transfigured by the active spiritual reality which discloses its presence and purpose in them. They are not merely physically inexplicable events, but astonishing and spiritually transforming signs of Divine presence, purpose and power. God brings such miracles about by a special intention to enable creatures to come to a more conscious and dynamic relation with him. At this point, David Hume's definition of miracles misses out precisely the most important thing: that they are intended to be disclosures of the Divine presence and foreshadowings of the Divine purpose for creation. Objects are not at all 'violated' in their proper natures. They are, perhaps for one transfiguring moment, taken beyond their natural powers in order to foreshadow their supernatural meaning and destiny. A miracle, as an extraordinary act of God, essentially has the character of a communication, possessing an intended meaning which is to be discerned by those who apprehend it in faith.

Miracles have a semiotic dimension; that is, they are intended by God to convey a meaning of great importance for the human spiritual quest. In a universe created by God to realize his purpose of bringing into being a community of rational creatures attaining eternal bliss by knowing and loving him, it would be strange indeed if no miracles occurred. For in this universe, creation by its nature finds fulfilment in a reality beyond and undergirding it. A miracle is an event which provides a vital clue to the nature of that fulfilment, to the means of achieving it, and to the character of the one who makes it possible. If there really is a God, the occurrence of some such physically highly improbable events becomes overall highly probable. A miracle is not adequately characterized as a transgression of a law of nature by a God or spirit. It is the raising of an object beyond its natural powers of operation, so as to show its supernatural origin, foundation and goal.

2.3 Signs and wonders?

John Marsh, *The Gospel of St John,* **Harmondsworth, Penguin, 1968, pp. 61–5**

The synoptic gospels recount many more 'miracles' than John, and the undiscerning reader might well see the picture of Jesus which emerges as that of a uniquely powerful thaumaturgist [*worker of wonders*]. If so, a reading of John might well put him right, and he could return to the synoptics and realize that his previous interpretation was wrong. For the synoptists, no less than John, saw Christ's miracles, and intended their readers to see them, as evidence for the divine nature of the Lord.

First it is made clear that the miracles are a sign that with Jesus' activity in miracles the age of fulfilment has at last arrived. What Isaiah foretold, 'In that day the deaf shall hear the words of the book, and out of their gloom and darkness the eyes of the blind shall see. The meek shall obtain fresh joy in the Lord, and the poor among men shall exult in the Holy One of Israel' (Isa. 29:18–19), is taken up into Jesus' own account of his mission: 'Go and tell John what you hear and see: the blind receive their sight and the lame walk, lepers are cleansed and the deaf hear, and the dead are raised up, and the poor have good news preached to them' (Matthew 11:5). The great messianic age has dawned in fulfilment of its promise in the life and actions of Jesus. Further, it is evident to observant readers of the synoptics that many of the wonders done by Jesus are really activities peculiar to God alone. That Jesus of Nazareth performed such deeds of divinity was itself a testimony to his divine nature. Thus it was Yahweh [*the personal name of God, as revealed to Moses*] who 'made the storm be still, and the waves of the sea were hushed' (Psalm 107:29); and it was Jesus who said 'Peace! Be still!' and the winds ceased and there was a great calm (Mark 4:39). Again, Jesus took it upon himself to proclaim the forgiveness of sins, a prerogative that every Jew believed to belong to God alone: and even Christ's adversaries recognized this: 'When Jesus saw their faith he said to the paralytic, "My son, your sins are forgiven". Now some of the scribes were sitting there, questioning in their hearts, "Why does this man speak thus? Who can forgive sins but God alone?"' (Mark 2:5–7). And while the Pharisees could number among themselves those who could exorcize demons, Jesus claims that he exorcizes them 'by God's finger', and that therefore the Kingdom of God had come upon men (Luke 11:14–20). Similarly for the Jew it was God who gave or permitted health or disease, life or death; that Jesus so manifestly had powers both to restore diseased bodies to health and even to quicken those that were dead is eloquent testimony to the synoptists' intention that he should be regarded not as a mere miracle worker, but rather as the embodiment in one personal human life of a worthy bearer of the name Immanuel, God is with us.

John's purpose is in the end the same. He uses different methods, notably in his treatment of miracles. Indeed John does not talk of 'miracles' but of *signs*. It has already become clear that to use such a word of the miracles of Jesus even as reported in the synoptic gospels would not be an entirely inappropriate thing: no doubt John was aware of this kind of consideration. But for John the works of Jesus are signs in a special way. It is possible to draw a distinction between 'external' and 'internal' signs; an 'external' sign would be something almost arbitrary, as, for example, the colour red as the sign on the hoods of some graduates of Oxford University that their degree is in the faculty of arts: any other colour, historical antecedents apart, would serve equally well. An 'internal' sign is not arbitrary, but in some way an actual part of the thing signified: as, for example, a candidate's examination paper is taken to be a 'sign' of the quality and extent of his knowledge, which cannot all be displayed in any one paper, or set of papers, but which nevertheless enables the examiner to judge fairly about the whole, of which he has only seen a part. The miracles in John are signs in this latter sense. They bring into the particular occasions of Jesus' ministry the reality they represent, which is always the same – his victorious self-offering on the cross. This can be seen in the very first sign, when the water of Jewish purification was changed by Jesus' presence into wine, which in its sacramental significance stated that in the self-offering on the cross there would be provided the one means of real purification which Judaism had sought, but failed, to provide. The working of the miracles is an 'impossibility' for the modern mind, but what most needs to be said is that however baffling to human reason the story of water into wine may be, the reality of that which is but a sign is even more amazing and 'impossible' – that the Word, creative, divine, eternal, should become flesh, and give himself in suffering and in death to make manifest in history the love and glory of God.

. . .

But if at last the 'awkward' question be faced: did the impossible occur?, the answer has to be that the central part of the Christian gospel to which every part of the gospels refers is itself impossible! The impossible went on in what took place: God was in Christ, reconciling the world to himself. The word became flesh and dwelt among us, and we beheld his glory. He came that we might have life, and have it abundantly. If that central 'impossibility' be believed, then it is less difficult to suppose that even in what took place there would be some uniquely remarkable signs of what was going on. . . . [I]nstead of having to say of a miracle that it 'breaks the laws of nature' (a notion equally repugnant to the critical inquiring mind and to the Christian understanding of God) it is possible to think that it simply goes outside the familiar pattern that men know, but only for the sake of the ultimate pattern, which is the whole purpose of God. God, that is to say, has a pattern for his world. The existence of evil, itself a mystery to man, creates distortions of that divine pattern. What God has done in Jesus Christ, and this includes the so-called miracles, is to restore the over-all pattern by some further departure from its familiar regularities.

It is, of course, quite possible for a man to accept the witness of John and the synoptics to the person and mission of Jesus, and not to wish to assert that any miracles took place. It is by no means necessary to make belief in Jesus Christ rest upon an acceptance of the miracles as 'observable history'. Indeed the contrary is true: truly Christian belief in the gospel miracles is possible only to those who have a belief in Jesus as Son of God and Saviour, for only those see the miracles as 'signs' of his real nature and mission. There is however no necessary intellectual dishonesty in believing in Jesus and denying the miracles, even if a previous acceptance of the miraculous led to a belief in Christ. The attainment of direct personal relationship with Jesus Christ by any means is properly so satisfying and self-authenticating that the instruments by which the relationship might be begun or explained cease to be of decisive importance. There are more ways than one for a Christian to live with intellectual integrity in the modern world.

Rowan A. Greer, *The Fear of Freedom: A Study of Miracles in the Roman Imperial Church*, University Park, PA, Pennsylvania State University Press, 1989, pp. 44–5

Augustine repeats the theme, already familiar to us, that even though Christ's miracles ought to produce faith in the incarnate Lord, they as often as not fail to do so. Indeed, people can believe in Christ without seeing any miracles at all. The Samaritans, for Augustine, are the paradigm example. In Galilee only Christ's few disciples believe in him because of the miracle at Cana (John 2:11), and the ruler in Cana believed only after he had confirmed the miracle by confirming the hour of his son's healing with the hour of Christ's promise to him.

. . .

Augustine certainly does not wish to deny the reality or the importance of miracles, but he is concerned that they be related to a deeper spiritual meaning. The 'greater works' mentioned by Christ (John 5:20) are to raise the dead, something greater than healing the sick. . . . [But] the true significance of Christ's raising the dead is not found in the physical miracle. After all, Lazarus, though brought back to life, is doomed to die like everyone else. The message for Augustine's congregation is both moral and spiritual:

Rise in thy heart; go forth from thy tomb. For thou wast lying dead in thy heart as in a tomb, and pressed down by the weight of evil habit as by a stone. Rise, and go forth. What is Rise and go forth? Believe and confess. For he that has believed has risen; he that confesses is gone forth.

Benedicta Ward, *Miracles and the Medieval Mind: Theory, Record and Event 1000–1215*, London, Scolar Press, 1982, p. 216

From the time of Augustine and Gregory the Great [*died AD 604*], there was in certain writers a concentration on the significance of miracles rather than on their marvellousness. Miracles were understood in the setting of a world that was seen as an extension of man and not apart from him, his desires, and his needs. Over against this unified creation was a world within a world, the 'mystic heaven' of God and the saints and miracles were one kind of connection between the two. The immense influence of Gregory the Great in formulating this fundamental medieval world view cannot be overstated, and it is being increasingly discussed by both historians and theologians. In his picture of St Benedict of Nursia in the *Dialogues*, praying in his cell and beholding the whole world gathered up in a single ray of light, Gregory was recording no mere wonder; it is an image of the union of man with God in, as he says, an 'inner light' that gave the perspective of heaven to the whole of creation. This ability to see reality in its totality as created and re-created by God removed miracles from the realm of simplistic wonder tales. In their Christian context they were signs of humanity redeemed, signs of the last age, of the ending of time in the single moment of redemption to which all things were to be related. On a more popular level, St Gregory offered men that most reassuring of all miracles – the glory of God revealed in the faces of the saints. The world was the antechamber of heaven, and he made sure that his readers understood that they had friends at court who would intercede for them in their needs and difficulties. This familiarity with the saints and the increasing desire to be in physical, practical contact with them by visiting the place where their bodies lay created the great shrines and pilgrimage routes of the Middle Ages. These remained, in however distant and confused a way, an image of men within the household of faith, exiles continually returning to their home country of heaven. In this context, the miracles of the saints were simply the ordinary life of heaven made manifest in earthly affairs, chinks in the barriers between heaven and earth, a situation in which not to have miracles was a cause of surprise, terror, and dismay.

David E. Jenkins, *God, Miracle and the Church of England,* London, SCM, 1987, pp. 4–5, 26–30

God, in order to declare and achieve our salvation, chose to become one of us. Jesus was the man God chose to become, and this Jesus, as a man, chose to die in obedience to his Father for the sake of God's kingdom and, as we have come to know, for us women and men and our salvation. This implies and expresses a truly wonderful and utterly gracious identification of God with us. God put himself at our disposal that we might be brought to his disposal. If God is this sort of loving, identifying and gracious God, then surely we must be very careful, reverent and reticent about how we pin certain sorts of miracles on him.

The choice of physical miracles with what might be called laser-beam-like precision and power would not seem to be a choice which he cared, or would care, to use. For if such a physical transformation with precision and power is an option open to God consistent with his purposes of creation, freedom and love, then we are faced with a very terrible dilemma indeed. We are faced with the claim that God is prepared to work knock-down physical miracles in order to let a select number of people into the secret of his incarnation, resurrection and salvation, but he is not prepared to use such methods in order to deliver from Auschwitz, prevent Hiroshima, overcome famine or bring about a blood-less transformation of apartheid. Such a God is surely a cultic idol. That is to say, he is a false and misdeveloped picture of the true and gracious God drawn up by would-be worshippers who have gone dangerously and sadly astray. If such a God is not a cultic idol produced by mistaken and confused worshippers, but actually exists, then he must be the very devil. For he prefers a few selected worshippers to all the sufferers of our world. Such a God is certainly not worth believing in. But I do not believe that we can possibly so have learned Christ.

. . .

As yet the ordinary life of the ordinary churches has scarcely begun to face up to the simple realities of 'the Bible in the modern world'. People seem unable even to begin to make the imaginative effort which is required to bridge the gap between the first-century honest and com-mitted witnesses who told their stories (and indeed similar honest witnesses in the third century, the fifth century or even the fourteenth century) and honest and committed seekers after truth from the scientific and industrial revolution onwards who are striving to produce accurate and effective historical and scientific reports. It is apparently taken for granted that writers of the New Testament must have supposed that they were giving what *we* call accurate and historical reports when they preached, recollected and wrote down the stories about Jesus. This is quite clearly a simple mistake. Recollected stories (themselves shaped and elaborated through several decades of telling) were set down in absolutely good faith to convey to current hearers and readers the dynamic truths about Jesus and his and our relationship to God. These were and are truths which are the essence of the gospel and the heart of the literally life-and-death matter of the resurrection faith. The truth could be conveyed by telling the same story in different ways, locating it in different places and giving it different details and applications. There is no more reason to suppose that the Gospel stories are any more like newspaper reports or scientific papers than, say, the first life of St. Cuthbert was. Authors of deep and passionate faith and commitment to a living realism and truth were witnessing in the manner proper to them and known to their times and their ways to what they knew and believed and were passionately convinced about. So to apply modern critical principles to biblical stories and to find differing layers of historicity, myth, legend and sheer embroidery is in no way to call in question either the total good faith and credibility of the writers or the validity and authenticity of their witness. They are simply doing it in their way – which is the way God always works through. Now we have to rely on the same God to make the witness, the truth and life-and-death matters of salvation powerful in our day and our way.

It is clear, as I say, that at the moment the church and the churches cannot become publicly, simply and peacefully adapted to a working recognition of this, but it is necessary to state it clearly and forcefully in a consideration of miracles. Otherwise the consideration is constantly confused by a misplaced argument of the sort: 'But you must believe in miracles like this which happen in this particular way because otherwise you are making Gospel writers liars or cheats or dupes.' This type of argument is wholly without weight and carries any force it has from a psychological problem about appreciating and appropriating the differences between thinking and feeling about truth and the world (and indeed ourselves) before the scientific and industrial revolutions and after them. The vital point is that the God in whom we believe is one and the same God throughout and it is *now* that we have to seek to perceive his presence and his signs in the terms and conditions which he allows us to live in. We cannot be transported back in a biblical escape machine and it is a denial of the God of the Bible to want this. He is always the contemporary God who is working for the future. *That* is the biblical God.

Thus a consideration of miracles requires us to ask how we can expect to find signs and wonders now within the mystery of God's dealing with the world which remains his world and remains the world within which he is active to be in touch and to save. This is where faith in Jesus as the Christ of God bears most directly on a consideration of, and even a discovery of, miracles. The crucial point is this: How does God exercise his power, reveal his presence, establish his possibilities and promises? It seems too often to be assumed that because, if he is God, he is 'God Almighty', he must do this, at least on significant occasions, in what I have come to call 'knock-down ways'. The basic picture, implied or explicit, is of God the Almighty King – and, since Constantine, of God the Almighty Emperor. And the point about such a cosmic king or emperor is that he is all-mighty, and being all-mighty means being wholly irresistible in a knock-down, take it or leave it, irresistible way. A miracle is then thought of as, so to speak, a localized and controlled explosion of that sort of power. This is God being irresistibly God and making clear that he is irrefutably God. Along this way of thinking miracle becomes, or can become, the principal evidence that God exists and that he is God. Look – *God* did that – it is a great and mighty wonder (even in a strictly localized and limited case) – it is too wonderful to have been done by any other power – therefore God did it – which proves to all that have eyes to see that God is – and indeed is God. But, if we really and truly take with utter seriousness the Christian symbol and doctrine of the Trinity, is this line of thinking properly open to us?

Let us suppose we believe – as I do – that Jesus of Nazareth is the Christ of God and therefore rightly recognized and proclaimed by the church as 'of one substance with the Father', as the Creed of Nicaea declares. This means that Jesus of Nazareth is God in the same sense as God the Father is God. . . . What does this say about the exercise of God's all-mightiness in the world, through the world and for the world? Surely it says that God is not an Imperial Caesar God of knock-down power but a creative servant God of invincible love. Because we fear freedom, are not yet ready for the totally mutual interdependence of love and do not yet have enough faith to be other than appalled at the risky nature of freely creating love and the alarmingly fragile, although amazingly existing, universe that this has allowed to come into being, we tend to want a God who is in control after the fashion of Caesar, so we construct religions which do exactly what Freud, Marx and Durkheim say they do – meet our psychological needs, support our vested interests and provide bonds for our highly imperfect societies. We do not have a God who is in control after the fashion of Caesar. We have a God who is creating control after the fashion of Christ. At least, so it seems to me if one is really trying to be a disciple of Jesus Christ.

The miracles, the communicating and encouraging signs and wonders which are the authentic miracles of God and of his Christ will not therefore be any or every member of the class of mystifying and wonder-making events which occur across the world for all sorts of reasons, objective and subjective, known and unknown. They will be those combinations of events, personal perceptions of events and presence of God which evoke that response of faith which is appropriate to the God the Father of our Lord Jesus Christ. This God has shown himself in Jesus, through Jesus and as Jesus, to be the creative power of holy, righteous and steadfast love committed to working through the world and to bringing out of the world the fulfilment of the sharing of his creativity and love. Miracles are part of encountering the openness and presence of God within the textures, structures and activities of the created world. They are produced and experienced by means of the space which is kept open, or made open, in that world by the intercourse of God with free and searching persons. This is why an authentic and genuinely revelatory miracle is always a mysterious combination of active and experiencing faith along with a sense of, and conviction about, a gift which goes beyond the ordinary, while experienced in and through the ordinary. There is always a way of interpreting or explaining a 'miracle' which does not oblige anyone to attribute it to God. To put it another way, miracles can be perceived and identified only by personal faith within the tradition, story and community of faith. But this does not mean that miracles are only subjective experiences. It means that God does not force himself on people. He offers himself to us for our response, obedience and collaboration.

2.4 Testing miracles

David Hume, 'Of Miracles', *An Enquiry Concerning the Human Understanding,* **1777, section X (reprinted in L. A. Selby-Bigge's edition, Oxford, Oxford University Press, 1902, pp. 110–11, 126–9)**

Though experience be our only guide in reasoning concerning matters of fact; it must be acknowledged, that this guide is not altogether infallible, but in some cases is apt to lead us into errors. One, who in our climate, should expect better weather in any week of June than in one of December, would reason justly, and conformably to experience; but it is certain, that he may happen, in the event, to find himself mistaken.

However, we may observe, that, in such a case, he would have no cause to complain of experience; because it commonly informs us beforehand of the uncertainty, by that contrariety of events, which we may learn from a diligent observation. All effects follow not with like certainty from their supposed causes. Some events are found, in all countries and all ages, to have been constantly conjoined together: Others are found to have been more variable, and sometimes to disappoint our expectations; so that, in our reasonings concerning matter of fact, there are all imaginable degrees of assurance, from the highest certainty to the lowest species of moral evidence.

A wise man, therefore, proportions his belief to the evidence. In such conclusions as are founded on an infallible experience, he expects the event with the last degree of assurance, and regards his past experience as a full *proof* of the future existence of that event. In other cases, he proceeds with more caution: He weighs the opposite experiments: He considers which side is supported by the greater number of experiments: to that side he inclines, with doubt and hesitation; and when at last he fixes his judgement, the evidence exceeds not what we properly call *probability*. All probability, then, supposes an opposition of experiments and observations, where the one side is found to overbalance the other, and to produce a degree of evidence, proportioned to the superiority. A hundred instances or experiments on one side, and fifty on another, afford a doubtful expectation of any event; though a hundred uniform experiments, with only one that is contradictory, reasonably beget a pretty strong degree of assurance. In all cases, we must balance the opposite experiments, where they are opposite, and deduct the smaller number from the greater, in order to know the exact force of the superior evidence.

. . .

I need not mention the difficulty of detecting a falsehood in any private or even public history, at the place, where it is said to happen; much more when the scene is removed to ever so small a distance. Even a court of judicature, with all the authority, accuracy, and judgement, which they can employ, find themselves often at a loss to distinguish between truth and falsehood in the most recent actions. But the matter never comes to any issue, if trusted to the common method of altercations and debate and flying rumours; especially when men's passions have taken part on either side.

In the infancy of new religions, the wise and learned commonly esteem the matter too inconsiderable to deserve their attention or regard.

And when afterwards they would willingly detect the cheat, in order to undeceive the deluded multitude, the season is now past, and the records and witnesses, which might clear up the matter, have perished beyond recovery.

No means of detection remain, but those which must be drawn from the very testimony itself of the reporters: and these, though always sufficient with the judicious and knowing, are commonly too fine to fall under the comprehension of the vulgar.

Upon the whole, then, it appears that no testimony for any kind of miracle has ever amounted to a probability, much less to a proof; and that, even supposing it amounted to a proof, it would be opposed by another proof; derived from the very nature of the fact, which it would endeavour to establish. It is experience only, which gives authority to human testimony; and it is the same experience, which assures us of the laws of nature. When, therefore, these two kinds of experience are contrary, we have nothing to do but substract the one from the other, and embrace an opinion, either on one side or the other, with that assurance which arises from the remainder. But according to the principle here explained, this substraction, with regard to all popular religions, amounts to an entire annihilation; and therefore we may establish it as a maxim, that no human testimony can have such force as to prove a miracle, and make it a just foundation for any such system of religion.

I beg the limitations here made may be remarked, when I say, that a miracle can never be proved, so as to be the foundation of a system of religion. For I own, that otherwise, there may possibly be miracles, or violations of the usual course of nature, of such a kind as to admit of proof from human testimony; though, perhaps, it will be impossible to find any such in all the records of history.

. . .

But should this miracle be ascribed to any new system of religion; men, in all ages, have been so much imposed on by ridiculous stories of that kind, that this very circumstance would be a full proof of a cheat, and sufficient, with all men of sense, not only to make them reject the fact, but even reject it without farther examination. Though the Being to whom the miracle is ascribed, be, in this case, Almighty, it does not, upon that account, become a whit more probable; since it is impossible for us to know the attributes or actions of such a Being, otherwise than from the experience which we have of his productions, in the usual course of nature. This still reduces us to past observation, and obliges us to compare the instances of the violation of truth in the testimony of men, with those of the violation of the laws of nature by miracles, in order to judge which of them is most likely and probable. As the violations of truth are more common in the testimony concerning religious miracles, than in that concerning any other matter of fact; this must diminish very much the authority of the former testimony, and make us form a general resolution, never to lend any attention to it, with whatever specious pretence it may be covered.

G. F. Woods, 'The Evidential Value of the Biblical Miracles', in C. F. D. Moule (ed.), *Miracles: Cambridge Studies in their Philosophy and History*, London, Mowbray, 1965, pp. 30–2

What, then, may be said in reply to the question whether the biblical miracles remain of equal evidential value for the truth of Christianity as in other days? As our knowledge of the natural order is not complete, it is not justifiable to say that miracles cannot take place. It is not logically unthinkable that they may take place. It may be thought highly improbable that they ever take place but no human mind is in a position to say that they cannot take place. For those who accept theism and for those who believe in the incarnation, it remains quite reasonable to approach sympathetically the accounts in the Bible of what are taken to be miracles done by the power of God. But it cannot be denied that the evidential value of the miraculous is closely interwoven with the metaphysical views of those to whom the evidence is offered. Those who reject theism and do not believe in the divinity of Christ have many alternative interpretations of the reported miracles. Theists and atheists, Christians and those who disbelieve Christianity, cannot avoid the intricate task of examining the historical probability of each account of what is said to be a miraculous event. This is an intricate matter because the weighing of historical evidence is affected by the metaphysical presuppositions of those who weigh the evidence. There are no metaphysically neutral scales. And, if the historical account of what is said to have been a miracle is accepted as broadly reliable, the question remains of judging whether the contemporary interpretation of the event as a divine miracle is true. At this point further problems arise. It does not now appear possible to determine the precise position of the frontier between the powers of man and the powers of God. What is thought to be beyond the powers of man need not necessarily be the work of God. It may be due to natural causes. It may have no cause at all. It may be the result of an impersonal supernatural cause or of a personal supernatural cause other than God. It may prove more profitable to study the miracle of divine grace operating in the personalities of sinful men than to attend exclusively to alleged miracles in the more physical order of nature. I think the moral criterion is more useful but it is hardly decisive in identifying a divine miracle. We cannot be quite sure that an unusual event is a divine miracle because it is congruous with a purpose which is morally worthy of approval. And there are moral problems associated with any view which suggests that a miracle can happen whenever the moral need for one is clear. Many of the problems in identifying divine miracles spring from the fundamental fact that the mind of man cannot fully comprehend the being and activity of God. The relation of God both to the natural order and to any miraculous events in the natural order is beyond our full understanding.

. . .

My own tentative conclusion is that the problem of the evidential value of the miraculous in support of the truth of the Christian faith is unlikely to receive a generally accepted solution for a very long time, if ever. In the meantime, it is a matter of balancing probabilities. This may sound a disappointing conclusion, but to accept probable evidence remains sensible where it is the best evidence available on matters where we cannot avoid making an explicit judgment or passing an implicit judgment in the action which we take or omit to take. We can still admire the sober wisdom of Bishop Joseph Butler who said, 'To us, probability is the very guide of life'.

Topics for discussion

1 How should theology define the concept of miracle?
2 Are miracles necessarily unfair? Can a God who allows Auschwitz also cure the lame and raise the dead?
3 How far should our current knowledge of medicine and the causes of illness affect the way we read the biblical miracles?
4 To what extent is it legitimate to detect symbolic meanings in the biblical narration of miracles, for example in St John's Gospel? Should such symbolic readings be seen as additional to the historical, or as alternative to it, in the original context or in our present context?
5 How theologically adequate is Tillich's account of miracle? Could a violation of a law of nature be included within it? How much is at stake for Christianity if a positive answer is denied or if it is accepted?
6 Could there ever be enough evidence to 'prove' a miracle?

3 Prayer

3.1 Prayer in the Bible

Genesis 28:18–22

28 [18]So Jacob rose early in the morning, and he took the stone that he had put under his head and set it up for a pillar and poured oil on the top of it. [19]He called that place Bethel; but the name of the city was Luz at the first. [20]Then Jacob made a vow, saying, 'If God will be with me, and will keep me in this way that I go, and will give me bread to eat and clothing to wear, [21]so that I come again to my father's house in peace, then the LORD shall be my God, [22]and this stone, which I have set up for a pillar, shall be God's house; and of all that you give me I will surely give one-tenth to you.'

Habakkuk 3:17–19

[17]**3** Though the fig tree does not blossom,
    and no fruit is on the vines;
  though the produce of the olive fails
    and the fields yield no food;
  though the flock is cut off from
      the fold
    and yet there is no herd in the stalls,
[18] yet I will rejoice in the LORD;
    I will exult in the God of my
      salvation.
[19] GOD, the Lord, is my strength;
    he makes my feet like the feet of a
      deer,
    and makes me tread upon the heights.

Psalm 34:1–10

1 I will bless the LORD at all times;
    his praise shall continually be in my
        mouth.
2 My soul makes its boast in the LORD;
    let the humble hear and be glad.
3 O magnify the LORD with me,
    and let us exalt his name together.

4 I sought the LORD, and he answered
        me,
    and delivered me from all my fears.
5 Look to him, and be radiant;
    so your faces shall never be
        ashamed.
6 This poor soul cried, and was heard by
        the LORD,
    and was saved from every trouble.
7 The angel of the LORD encamps
    around those who fear him, and
        delivers them.
8 O taste and see that the LORD is good;
    happy are those that take refuge in
        him.
9 O fear the LORD, you his holy ones,
    for those who fear him have no
        want.
10 The young lions suffer want and
        hunger,
    but those who seek the LORD lack
        no good thing.

Psalm 35:1–3, 26–28

1 Contend, O LORD, with those who
        contend with me;
    fight against those who fight
        against me!
2 Take hold of shield and buckler,
    and rise up to help me!

3 Draw the spear and javelin
  against my pursuers;
 say to my soul,
  'I am your salvation.'

          . . .

26 Let all those who rejoice at my
       calamity
   be put to shame and confusion;
  let those who exalt themselves against
       me
   be clothed with shame and
       dishonour.

27 Let those who desire my vindication
     shout for joy and be glad,
   and say evermore,
  'Great is the Lord,
     who delights in the welfare of his
       servant.'
28 Then my tongue shall tell of your
       righteousness
   and of your praise all day long.

Psalm 38:1–4, 17–22

1 O Lord, do not rebuke me in your
      anger,
   or discipline me in your wrath.
2 For your arrows have sunk into me,
     and your hand has come down
       on me.

3 There is no soundness in my flesh
     because of your indignation;
  there is no health in my bones
     because of my sin.
4 For my iniquities have gone over my
      head;
      they weigh like a burden too heavy
        for me.

          . . .

17 For I am ready to fall,
and my pain is ever with me.
18 I confess my iniquity;
I am sorry for my sin.
19 Those who are my foes without cause
are mighty,
and many are those who hate me
wrongfully.
20 Those who render me evil for good
are my adversaries because I follow
after good

21 Do not forsake me, O LORD;
O my God, do not be far from me;
22 make haste to help me,
O Lord, my salvation.

Psalm 86:1–13

1 Incline your ear, O LORD, and answer
me,
for I am poor and needy.
2 Preserve my life, for I am devoted to
you;
save your servant who trusts in you.
You are my God; ³be gracious to me,
O Lord,
for to you do I cry all day long.
4 Gladden the soul of your servant,
for to you, O Lord, I lift up my soul.
5 For you, O Lord, are good and
forgiving,
abounding in steadfast love to all
who call on you.
6 Give ear, O LORD, to my prayer;
listen to my cry of supplication.
7 In the day of my trouble I call on you,
for you will answer me.

8 There is none like you among the
gods, O Lord,
nor are there any works like yours.

9 All the nations you have made shall
       come
    and bow down before you, O Lord,
    and shall glorify your name.
10 For you are great and do wondrous
       things;
    you alone are God.
11 Teach me your way, O LORD,
    that I may walk in your truth;
    give me an undivided heart to
      revere your name,
12 I give thanks to you, O Lord my God,
    with my whole heart,
    and I will glorify your name for
      ever.
13 For great is your steadfast love
      towards me;
    you have delivered my soul from
      the depths of Sheol.

Matthew 6:5–15

6 5'And whenever you pray, do not be like the hypocrites; for they love to stand and pray in the synagogues and at the street corners, so that they may be seen by others. Truly I tell you, they have received their reward. 6But whenever you pray, go into your room and shut the door and pray to your Father who is in secret; and your Father who sees in secret will reward you.

7'When you are praying, do not heap up empty phrases as the Gentiles do; for they think that they will be heard because of their many words. 8Do not be like them, for your Father knows what you need before you ask him.

9 'Pray then in this way:
Our Father in heaven,
    hallowed be your name.
10   Your kingdom come.
    Your will be done,
      on earth as it is in heaven.
11   Give us this day our daily bread.

12   And forgive us our debts,
             as we also have forgiven
                  our debtors.
13   And do not bring us to the time of
             trial,
             but rescue us from the evil one.

¹⁴For if you forgive others their trespasses, your heavenly Father will also forgive you; ¹⁵ but if you do not forgive others, neither will your Father forgive your trespasses.

Luke 18:1–14

18 ¹Then Jesus told them a parable about their need to pray always and not to lose heart. ²He said, 'In a certain city there was a judge who neither feared God nor had respect for people. ³In that city there was a widow who kept coming to him and saying, "Grant me justice against my opponent." ⁴For a while he refused; but later he said to himself, "Though I have no fear of God and no respect for anyone, ⁵yet because this widow keeps bothering me, I will grant her justice, so that she may not wear me out by continually coming." ⁶And the Lord said, 'Listen to what the unjust judge says. ⁷And will not God grant justice to his chosen ones who cry to him day and night? Will he delay long in helping them? ⁸I tell you, he will quickly grant justice to them. And yet, when the Son of Man comes, will he find faith on earth?'

⁹He also told this parable to some who trusted in themselves that they were righteous and regarded others with contempt: ¹⁰'Two men went up to the temple to pray, one a Pharisee and the other a tax-collector. ¹¹The Pharisee, standing by himself, was praying thus, "God, I thank you that I am not like other people: thieves, rogues, adulterers, or even like this tax-collector. ¹²I fast twice a week; I give a tenth of all my income." ¹³But the tax-collector, standing far off, would not even look up to heaven, but was beating his breast and saying, "God, be merciful to me, a sinner!" ¹⁴I tell you, this man went down to his home justified rather than the other; for all who exalt themselves will be humbled, but all who humble themselves will be exalted.'

John 16:23–4

16 ²³'On that day you will ask nothing of me. Very truly, I tell you, if you ask anything of the Father in my name, he will give it to you. ²⁴Until now you have not asked for anything in my name. Ask and you will receive, so that your joy may be complete.'

Philippians 4:4–7

4 [4]Rejoice in the Lord always; again I will say, Rejoice. [5]Let your gentleness be known to everyone. The Lord is near. [6]Do not worry about anything, but in everything by prayer and supplication with thanksgiving let your requests be made known to God. [7]And the peace of God, which surpasses all understanding, will guard your hearts and your minds in Christ Jesus.

3.2 Prayer and pain

Johann Baptist Metz, 'Approaches to Prayer', in Johann Baptist Metz and Karl Rahner, *The Courage to Pray*, London, Burns & Oates, 1980, pp. 15–18

Praying is not an imaginary ladder enabling us to escape from our fears. Nor does it suppress or overcome our fears. First and foremost it permits fear. 'My soul is very sorrowful, even to death', Christ prayed in the Garden of Gethsemane (cf. Matt. 26:38). Fear is allowed in, not banished. Fear, sorrow and distress can easily provide the impetus to pray. Apathy has no part to play in prayer. The aim of prayer is not to protect us from pain or suffering. Nothing alarms us more than a person ostensibly devoid of fear. But is it not true that fear makes people malleable and unfree; that frightened people are precisely those most liable to be exploited by outside forces? We must be more specific. Only when fear is suppressed do we become unfree and manipulated; only then can fear constrict our hearts and render us incapable of conceiving our own anguish or that of those around us. By means of prayer, however, this fear can even make us free, just as Christ was freed by his fearful prayer of distress in the Garden of Olives.

Then there is *prayer induced by guilt*. Again prayer can prevent us from giving in to the web of excuses we weave around ourselves; it can help us cope with the misery of our guilty consciences. What can we feel if, reflecting on the past, we have to admit to ourselves that our lives are scattered with the ruins of people destroyed by our egoism? Faced with such a realization, what reaction could we have but an overwhelming desire to make amends? What alternative is there to despair but the plea for forgiveness and, according to the messianic light of hope, additional pleas precisely for those destroyed? This argument is of course open to the suspicion that our religious outcry in reaction to our own guilt amounts to a very subtle form of escapism, both from ourselves and from responsibility. . . .

The examples given above might possibly suggest that the way to prayer is through negative experiences, through pain, sorrow and distress, rather than through the positive influence of joy and gratitude. In reality, however, the active fight against overwhelming hopelessness, affirmation in the negative face of pain, is the outcome of a tremendously positive attitude. The experience of prayer I wish to underline here has a long tradition in the history of religion and especially in the history of our own faith. In history prayer is not limited to the expression of joy and exaltation; on the contrary, it also embraces the expression of fear and despair, a cry from the depths of the soul.

For this reason I should like to mention a danger which I feel is implicit in the customary language of prayer currently used by the Church. Perhaps not enough emphasis is laid on the pain of negativity? Perhaps our prayers are often much too positive and over-affirmative, resorting to clichés when referring to suffering and conflict and thus incapable of giving adequate expression to our acceptance of difficulties and crises? In my view this kind of prayer is symptomatic of weakness and despondency, and no longer entrusts our pain and the despair of our lives to God in prayer.

This tendency to be overly affirmative in our daily prayers is full of serious implications. It surely exacerbates our inarticulateness in pain and crises, depressing us further instead of giving us courage. How can people in dangerous situations, in pain or oppression, identify with prayers which use this kind of language?

3.3 Prayer and answers

Peter Baelz, *Prayer and Providence: A Background Study*, London, SCM, 1968, pp. 111–18

It is clear from what we have been saying that we expect prayer to make a difference to the man who prays – just as we should expect to see a difference in a man who stopped to think what he was doing, or in a man who fell in love. We have argued that there is a very proper sense in which we may speak of the activity of God engaging and eliciting a response of love and obedience in the depths of the human spirit. In communion with God a man comes to a new knowledge of himself and a new apprehension of the world around him. We have seen that this communion cannot be restricted to a private relationship between God and the individual, but moves towards a total vision of all things in harmonious response to God in fulfilment of the divine will and purpose, and issues in action which seeks to embody and express that will in the actual imperfect situation in which the individual finds himself. Thus we may speak of God's acting in the world through the response of the faithful. His activity in the world is mediated through man; it is, as it were, an indirect activity rather than a direct activity. For a faith which has its source in the belief that it was in and through a man that God wrought the salvation of the world, it is nothing surprising that the norm for our interpretation of God's response to prayer is to be found in his indwelling in human hearts and minds and his inspiration of human thought and action. Is this, however, the full measure of God's response? Does he answer our prayers only by helping us to help ourselves? Can he ever be said to do for us in the world what we cannot do for ourselves? The concerted witness of countless Christian believers reveals a conviction that God does just this, that there are in fact occasions when he answers prayer directly by granting what is asked. What are we to say in view of such a persistent belief?

Several objections even to the serious consideration of such a sugges-tion at once arise, objections which lie near the surface of our whole discussion and which emerge sharply just at this point.

First, it may be said that the whole idea of God's answering prayer by some special action in the world betrays an anthropomorphic and naturalistic concept of God, whose being is transcendent of this world and whose activity, if activity is the right word at all, is universal. To this we may reply that our use of the language of personal being in speaking of God, for which we have tried to give some justification, is bound to be anthropomorphic to some extent, simply because personal being is known to us through the exercise of it ourselves. With Lotze, however, we may hold that personal being is not necessarily limited being; and when we ascribe it to God we negate those limitations which are associated with it in our own human experiences. Thus, for example, when we pray to God for some particular benefit, there is no question of our informing God of certain things of which he was ignorant or forgetful, as if we were reminding an absent-minded professor that he was expected to be at a particular place to give a lecture which he had promised to deliver. 'Your heavenly Father knoweth that ye have need of all these things.' In St Augustine's words: 'God does not ask us to tell him our needs in order that he may learn about them, but in order that we may be made capable of receiving his gifts.'

. . .

Second, it may be said that the scientific view of the order of the world prevents our taking seriously the suggestion that an event in the world may be 'caused' by the immediate volition of God. To this far-reaching objection we shall content ourselves with a brief reply. If the scientific view of the order of the world can make room for human freedom and human volition without disrupting its own procedures, so too can it, in principle, make room for divine freedom and divine volition; for although it is impossible for us to know what the relation of God to the world is in itself or the way in which it is dependent upon his creative will, it is the relation of the human will to human behaviour that we look to for an analogy.

. . .

The third, and from the religious angle probably the most telling, objection is a moral one, what we may call the problem of distribution in the pattern of answered prayer. Suppose we allow that God acts directly in the world in answer to prayer. Can we, however, discern any coherent moral and spiritual pattern linking the occasions on which he grants a petition with those on which he refuses? Do we really see the working together of all things for good in both groups of occasions? Is it not more likely that what appear to be answers to our prayers are coincidental occurrences which would have happened anyhow, whether we had prayed or not? Are we convinced that God has good reason for granting in one instance what he refuses in another? There are few, I suspect, who would claim to see such rhyme and reason. They might do their best to distinguish between the different instances so as to account for God's differing responses. They might say that certain petitions were too trivial for God to grant, or that the supplicant had not sufficient faith and that because of this lack of faith God withheld his hand. But in the end they are likely simply to reassert their conviction that there must be such a pattern issuing from the divine wisdom in spite of their failure actually to discern it. God *is* a God who answers prayer when it accords with his wisdom and will, although we have to confess that we cannot fathom the depths of his wisdom or penetrate the mystery of his will.

. . .

In Christ's own response to God we discern two aspects. On the one hand, there is his acceptance of the limitation of the natural order. He is involved in the conditions of the world. He accepts its sufferings. In temptations he rejects the whole notion of invoking supernatural powers. Obedience to his Father's will leads him along the way of the cross. There is no escaping the agony and the pain. On the other hand, there streams through him the power of divine love. He heals the sick, he stills the storm. We may not know where to draw the line between the factual and the symbolic, but we are gripped with the sense that the achievements of Christ in obedient response to the love of God shatter our conceptions of what is natural and possible.

. . .

It is time to bring these tentative remarks to a conclusion. Perhaps it is a mistake to think of God's doing something in response to our prayer, as if our prayer had persuaded God to do what he could have done but refused to do without our praying for it. Perhaps we ought rather to think that our asking in faith may make it possible for God to do something which he could not have done without our asking. We may give the divine Love a *point d'appui* [*fulcrum*], so that through our prayer it may realize possibilities which only in this way it can actualize. Perhaps we must go on praying in the faith and hope that this is so, even though we cannot yet explain how it is so. In prayer we refuse to accept as ultimate what appear to be the fixed conditions of the world, because we believe that these conditions are not ultimate. They have a temporary validity within the purpose of God, but they are in the end subordinate to his love. We do not yet know what love can or cannot achieve. Our faith prompts us to pray, in Kierkegaard's phrase, even 'for the impossible'. Prayer 'is a form of expectation'. It is the growing point in the divine-human encounter. It is participation in new creation.

H. H. Price. *Essays in the Philosophy of Religion*, Oxford, Oxford University Press, 1972, pp. 42, 44–6, 50–1, 54–5

[*The author considers an agnostic who admits that petitionary prayer 'works' but offers a nontheistic explanation of 'how it works'.*]
First, he will draw our attention to the phenomena of self-suggestion. He will say that when we pray to God on our own behalf and ask that we may be given the courage or strength or intellectual enlightenment we need, we do quite often receive what we prayed for. But surely this can be explained by self-suggestion? It is true that the *idea* of God plays an important part in the process; but what reason is there to think that God himself has anything to do with it, if indeed there is such a being? The idea of God is just part of the psychological machinery which the praying person uses: its function is to make the self-suggestion more confident by 'personifying' our own unconscious powers.

. . .

But whatever we think of this self-suggestion theory of petitionary prayer, it will only apply, at the best, to the prayers which a person makes on his own behalf. Moreover, we notice that even when a person prays on his own behalf, and his prayer is answered, the answer often comes about through the actions of other people.

Suppose that you have promised to visit a friend in a town you have never been to before, and you get lost. It is Sunday evening and pouring with rain. There is no one about in the streets. You have no map of the town, or if you have, you forgot to bring it with you. All you know is that your friend's address is No. 15 Acacia Street. Then, if you are a very pious person, you may ask for God's help. 'Please, Lord, may I find Tom's house.'

There is indeed a tradition that when a person prays on his own behalf, he must ask only for 'spiritual' goods and not for 'temporal' ones, although when one is praying for another person one may ask for goods of either sort on his behalf. I doubt whether this tradition is supported by what we are told about prayer in the New Testament, but let us suppose that you accept it. Still, you did promise to visit your friend Tom this evening, and keeping one's promise presumably counts as a 'spiritual' good. So you have no scruples about making this petition. And then a few minutes later you see someone opening his front door to let the cat out. You ask him where Acacia Street is. He tells you to take the first turning on the right, and then the third turning on the left, and you get to your friend's house no more than ten minutes late.

Was it just a coincidence that the man happened to let the cat out at that particular time? Conceivably it might be. But one should consider a remark made by Archbishop Temple: 'When I pray, coincidences begin to happen.' This seems to me a good way of stating the problem. Any one case in which a person receives what he prays for might be a coincidence. But if this sort of thing happens quite frequently in the lives of persons who pray (and the testimony of religious people is that it does) here is a fact which needs explanation.

What could the explanation be? Are we to say that when you received what you asked for, this came about by a kind of *ad hoc* divine intervention, whereby the man was 'made' to let the cat out just at the time when you were passing, though he would not otherwise have done so? Or perhaps you were 'made' to walk at such a speed that you would reach the spot just when the cat was being let out?

This might be described as the 'miraculous' theory of the way petitionary prayers are answered. It would amount to saying that God works a kind of minor miracle on the praying person's behalf. I do not wish to maintain that miracles never happen. But if one may venture to say so, they would cease to be miraculous if they happened all day and every day. A miracle is by definition something exceptional, 'extraordinary' in the literal sense of the word; and this is still true if the miracle is, so to speak, a very little one.

. . .

It seems to me better, and indeed more consonant with a theistic view of the world, to say that we should revise our views of what the laws of nature are. And *a fortiori* that is the line which an irreligious person must take. [T]he question I am asking is, can he give a non-theistic explanation of the fact that petitionary prayers are often answered? . . . We can now see that the phenomena of self-suggestion, important as they are, will not give the [agnostic] all he wants. At the very most, they will only enable him to explain how prayers on one's behalf are answered, and not even all of these. For as I have pointed out already, when one prays for help for oneself, and receives it, the help may very well come through the actions of other people.

It seems to me, then, that . . . [he] had better take some account of the phenomena investigated by psychical researchers, paranormal or parapsychological phenomena. The most relevant of these, and perhaps the best established, is telepathy.

. . .

We can now propose a revised version of the self-suggestion theory of petitionary prayer. There were two difficulties in that theory. The first was that one may pray on behalf of other persons, and it seems that such prayers are answered sufficiently often to make this practise well worth while. The second difficulty was that even when a person prays on his own behalf, for deliverance from some trouble of his own, or for strength or guidance or intellectual enlightenment which he himself needs, his prayer is often answered through the actions of other people. Could we get over these difficulties by saying that the 'self', to which the suggestion is made, is not the individual self of you or me, but the Common Unconscious which somehow 'underlies' the individual minds of us all?

. . .

But will [this] satisfy a religious person who knows by first-hand experience 'what it feels like' to pray? I am sure it will not, if his religion is of the theistic type, though if he is a Buddhist, conceivably it might. But a

Christian, or indeed any theist, will object that this telepathic theory of petitionary prayer leaves something out: the personal relationship between man and God. He will insist that prayer is not just thinking, nor even wishing; it is *asking*. An 'I-thou' relation is an essential part of it. In petitionary prayer we are *addressing* one whom we love and trust, and we are sure that he loves us.

Is there any way of reconciling these two views of petitionary prayer, the psychical researcher's view and the theistic view? Or is a theist after all compelled to maintain that whenever our prayers are answered God works a minor miracle at our request? That would be a very unwelcome conclusion for the theist himself, even perhaps a self-contradictory one; for, as I have suggested already, if miracles were always happening, hundreds or even thousands of them every day, there would no longer be any meaning in calling them 'miracles'.

But I think the theist has another alternative. He might say, instead, that when and if we sincerely place ourselves in this 'I-thou' relationship with God, and make our requests to him, the very fact that we do so 'releases' paranormal forces of some kind, and these in their turn bring about the result which we asked for. If so, there is after all nothing *ad hoc* or miraculous about the way our prayers are answered. Instead, the request itself, if we make it in the appropriate 'I-thou' manner, brings about the conditions which are necessary for its fulfilment.

Fraser Watts, *Theology and Psychology*, Aldershot, Ashgate, 2002, pp. 108–9

I want to explore the contribution that ideas of 'resonance' or 'tuning' can make as additional metaphors to set alongside that of divine action. [*Resonance occurs when an object vibrates with its natural frequency when subjected to the influence of an external source of a similar frequency.*] In discussing how prayer can be understood in relation to science, John Polkinghorne refers to 'the tuning of divine and human wills to mutual resonance through the collaboration of prayer'. He explicates the notion of resonance by referring to the 'coherence' of laser light, in which oscillations are perfectly in step with one another, thereby affording maximum reinforcement. Alternatively, less technically, one might think of resonance in terms of people being 'attuned' to God, rather as a receiver can be attuned to a transmitter. Of course, the concept of resonance does not exclude all notion of 'action'; in physical resonance there is still a specific 'input'. However, the metaphors of 'resonance', 'tuning' or 'coherence' seem to point in helpful directions.

Above all, they suggest the interactive nature of God's influence on human beings, something which is especially important in considering how the Spirit acts in relation to people. For the Spirit to act, there has to be receptivity. In the Johannine metaphor, the Spirit comes to 'dwell' with believers; and this dwelling requires receptiveness. The metaphors of resonance, tuning, and coherence also suggest how God normally acts in relation to people, allowing them the freedom either to respond, or to go their own way. The notion of resonance is essentially an interactive notion, which is what is required when we consider God's action in relation to people.

Further, there is an implication of constancy in the way God seeks to bring us into attunement with himself. The Christian tradition has generally emphasized that God does not seek to reach out to people and guide them only at certain times, but constantly seeks to do so, even where there is no receptivity on the part of the people to whom he reaches out. The human world, reflecting as it does God's creative purpose, is one in which people's thoughts and actions are constantly being drawn into attunement with God's nature and purpose.

Nevertheless, the notion of resonance also implies that, on specific occasions, when we become attuned to God, new possibilities are opened up which might not otherwise arise. In this way, the resonance metaphor is not at all inconsistent with 'mighty acts of God' occurring, once resonance is established. Resonance thus implies a link between general providence and special providence. This is to be welcomed in view of the fact that the notion of special providence becomes particularly problematic when it is divorced from general providence.

Thinking about God's providence in terms of resonance and attunement is also helpful in suggesting the right kind of relationship between providence and other causal processes. There are two pitfalls to be avoided here. One is to see divine action simply as no more than a particular, religious way of describing events in the world, but one with no real explanatory power, and which reflects no actual divine influence. Liberal theologians have often been tempted by that kind of approach (for example, Maurice Wiles). The other is to see God's influence as real, but operating in a way that is totally divorced from all other causal influences in the world. If talk of resonance is to be fruitful, it needs to point us towards a way of conceptualizing God's influential presence in the world that recognizes it as real, but preserves an interactive compatibility between God's influence and other levels of explanation.

The metaphor of resonance is, of course, fairly close to talk about the input of 'information' from God (for example, Arthur Peacocke). This is an attractive idea, and has the possible advantage of not implying an input of physical energy. However, there are at least two potential problems with it. If 'information' does not involve physical energy, there remains a 'causal joint' problem of how it relates to physical energy. Also, at least in the form in which informational input has been proposed so far, it seems to place a less clear emphasis on human receptivity than does the idea of resonance. However, there may not ultimately be much at stake here. If the concept of information-input is adopted in preference to that of resonance, I suggest that it will be important to develop it in a way that is more explicitly interactive.

Vincent Brümmer, *What Are We Doing When We Pray? A Philosophical Inquiry*, London, SCM, 1984, pp. 33–4

It is clear that the practice of impetratory prayer [*prayers of request aimed at 'getting things by praying for them'*] presupposes a *personal* God who can freely choose to do certain things even though he has the ability to do otherwise. Only such things have the two-way contingency necessary for them to be the sort of things which could meaningfully be the objects of petition.

A second presupposition which is also constitutive for impetratory prayer, is that God does what he is asked *because* he is asked. In this sense the petition itself is a *condition* for God's doing what he is requested. On the one hand, however, it is not a *sufficient* condition making it inevitable for God to comply with the request. In that case prayer would become a kind of magical technique by which God could be manipulated by us, and we would no longer approach him as a rational agent who acts from free choice. On the other hand, although the petition is not a *cause* which makes God's response inevitable, it is the *reason* for his response: God does what he does *because* he is asked. In this sense the request is a *necessary* condition for God's doing what he is asked. ' "God brought about situation S because of X's prayers" implies "If X had not prayed, or had prayed otherwise, God would not have brought about situation S" ' (Peter Geach, *God and the Soul*, London, Routledge & Kegan Paul, 1969, pp. 88–9).

In the light of this analysis it again becomes clear that the practice of impetratory prayer presupposes a *personal* view of God. Like human persons, God is taken to be a rational agent. But God is also very different from human persons, with the result that various conceptual problems have traditionally been raised in connection with impetratory prayer. These problems have led many to doubt whether petitionary prayer could meaningfully be interpreted as impetratory. Are the expressive and therapeutic functions of petitionary prayer not sufficient to justify this practice in religion? . . . These problems have to do with the various ways in which God differs from human persons: Unlike us, he is immutable, omniscient, perfectly good and a transcendent agent.

3.4 Prayer, determinism and freedom

C. S. Lewis, *Miracles: A Preliminary Study*, London, HarperCollins, 1974, pp. 178, 182–4

I find it very difficult to conceive an intermediate class of events which are neither miraculous nor merely 'ordinary.' Either the weather at Dunkirk was or was not that which the previous physical history of the universe, by its own character, would inevitably produce. If it was, then how is it 'specially' providential? If it was not, then it was a miracle.

It seems to me, therefore, that we must abandon the idea that there is any special class of events (apart from miracles) which can be distinguished as 'specially providential.' Unless we are to abandon the conception of Providence altogether, and with it the belief in efficacious prayer, it follows that all events are equally providential. If God directs the course of events at all then he directs the movement of every atom at every moment; 'not one sparrow falls to the ground' without that direction. The 'naturalness' of natural events does not consist in being somehow outside God's providence. It consists in their being interlocked with one another inside a common space-time in accordance with the fixed pattern of the 'laws.'

. . .

Most of our prayers if fully analysed, ask either for a miracle or for events whose foundations will have to have been laid before I was born, indeed, laid when the universe began. But then to God (though not to me) I and the prayer I make in 1945 were just as much present at the creation of the world as they are now and will be a million years hence. God's creative act is timeless and timelessly adapted to the 'free' elements within it: but this timeless adaptation meets our consciousness as a sequence of prayer and answer.

Two corollaries follow:

1. People often ask whether a given event (not a miracle) was really an answer to a prayer or not. I think that if they analyse their thought they

will find they are asking, 'Did God bring it about for a special purpose or would it have happened anyway as part of the natural course of events?' But this (like the old question, 'Have you left off beating your wife?') makes either answer impossible. In the play, *Hamlet*, Ophelia climbs out on a branch overhanging a river: the branch breaks, she falls in and drowns. What would you reply if anyone asked, 'Did Ophelia die because Shakespeare for poetic reasons wanted her to die at that moment – or because the branch broke?' I think one would have to say, 'For both reasons.' Every event in the play happens as a result of other events in the play, but also every event happens because the poet wants it to happen. All the events in the play are Shakespearian events; similarly all events in the real world are providential events. All events in the play, however, come about (or ought to come about) by the dramatic logic of events. Similarly all events in the real world (except miracles) come about by natural causes. 'Providence' and Natural causation are not alternatives; both determine every event because both are one.

2. When we are praying about the result, say, of a battle or a medical consultation the thought will often cross our minds that (if only we knew it) the event is already decided one way or the other. I believe this to be no good reason for ceasing our prayers. The event certainly has been decided – in a sense it was decided 'before all worlds.' But one of the things taken into account in deciding it, and therefore one of the things that really cause it to happen, may be this very prayer that we are now offering. Thus, shocking as it may sound, I conclude that we can at noon become part causes of an event occurring at ten a.m. (Some scientists would find this easier than popular thought does.) The imagination will, no doubt, try to play all sorts of tricks on us at this point. It will ask, 'Then if I stop praying can God go back and alter what has already happened?' No. The event has already happened and one of its causes has been the fact that you are asking such questions instead of praying. It will ask, 'Then if I begin to pray can God go back and alter what has already happened?' No. The event has already happened and one of its causes is your present prayer. Thus something does really depend on my choice. My free act contributes to the cosmic shape. That contribution is made in eternity or 'before all worlds'; but my consciousness of contributing reaches me at a particular point in the time-series.

The following question may be asked: If we can reasonably pray for an event which must in fact have happened or failed to happen several hours ago, why can we not pray for an event which we know *not* to have happened? e.g. pray for the safety of someone who, as we know, was killed yesterday. What makes the difference is precisely our knowledge. The known event states God's will. It is psychologically impossible to pray for what we know to be unobtainable; and if it were possible the prayer would sin against the duty of submission to God's known will.

Peter Geach, *God and the Soul*, London, Routledge and Kegan Paul, 1969, pp. 90–1, 96–7

Fortunately we need not discuss the mysteries of God's eternal knowledge and power in order to see that Lewis's theory will not do. For it is not a matter of what God knows and can do, but of what we in prayer can sensibly say. If a prayer does not make good sense, then equally it does not make good sense to speak of God's granting it. And a prayer certainly does not make sense if we try to use a past tense of the imperative mood and pray that a state of affairs *may have* come about. In using the imperative we represent the situation as still to be brought about, and in using the past tense we represent it as already a *fait accompli* one way or the other. These representations will not fit together; such a prayer makes no better sense than a schoolboy's prayer for π to have the [incorrect] value he gave it in his maths test . . .

Lewis admits that it is no good praying for a thing not to have happened when we know it has happened; for in that case we should be setting our own will against God's will as manifested in the actual issue. But if my own objection to praying about the past is a sound one, then it is not a matter of our ignorance, any more than it is a matter of God's omniscience. A prayer for something to have happened is simply an absurdity, regardless of the utterer's knowledge or ignorance of how things actually went; just as the prayer for π to have a certain numerical value is absurd, whether or not the schoolboy has learned the actual value of π after doing the test.

I am not arguing that an imperative in the perfect tense never occurs in ordinary language or is necessarily meaningless . . . [W]e get such an imperative when a tutor says to his pupil 'Have your essay written by Tuesday morning'. But this does not make sense of the sort of imperative that would be used in praying about the past. The indicative corresponding to the tutor's imperative is 'You will have written your essay by Tuesday morning'; and this is not in the past tense. It is in the tense aptly called by old grammarians *'paulo post futurum'*: it relates to a time somewhere between the time of speaking and the following Tuesday morning – and thus to a time which is future, not past, when the tutor speaks, though by the Tuesday morning it will be a past time.

Now suppose the tutor had said: 'Have your essay written by last Tuesday morning'. The undergraduate could make no sense of this; there is no coherently constructible indicative to correspond. For 'You will have written your essay by last Tuesday morning', read so as to correspond to this imperative, implies a contradictory time-specification, of a time which is both future at the time of speaking and past by the previous Tuesday morning. And it is equally incoherent to pray to God 'Let my friend's aeroplane not have crashed last Tuesday morning' – supposing that I've just learned my friend was flying that day, but have not learned whether he landed safely. No doubt God, who knows our necessities before we ask and our ignorance in asking, sometimes does in his mercy do *something* about the most confused prayer; but there's no sense in saying he *grants* such a prayer.

· · ·

The empty claim that all events in the material world are determined in their causes and are 'in principle' predictable has had a deplorable influence on Christian apologetic; although men of science today are less confident about this claim than a man like Tyndall was, the mischief has already been done by their predecessors. It is often held with absolute certainty that events in the material world (at any rate large-scale events) are determined in certain created causes, so that (to use C. S. Lewis's example) the fair weather at the evacuation of Dunkirk was determinate at the formation of the solar system. Sometimes this certainly is based on a superstitious belief in the predictive feats of science – really, of course, a physicist cannot predict how dice will fall any better then I can. Sometimes, people appeal to a supposed metaphysical truth, 'the principle of causality', which is alleged to rule out a two-way contingency. Those who thus swear by 'the principle of causality' are rarely forthcoming with any attempt at an exact statement of it; but I well remember one of them having a shot at this in discussion, and coming up with a formulation essentially like Spinoza's, which had the undesired consequence of ruling out all free choice, Divine as well as human.

We often find Christian apologists committing themselves to strict determinism as regards the material world (at least in its large-scale aspects) and then by consequence to the desperate task of explaining how God, while 'binding Nature fast in fate / Left free the human will'. *Pace* Pope and Leibniz, I think the thing cannot be done. If Nature is bound fast in fate, then the human will is a chimera buzzing in a vacuum and feeding upon second intentions. How can I have any freedom of speech if the sound-waves impinging on your ears as I speak are determined in material causes going back to the origins of the solar system and having nothing to do with my thoughts and intentions? It is indeed a presupposition of rational human action that there should be a great deal of determinism in the material world; otherwise . . . we should be like Alice trying to play croquet with a live hedgehog as a ball and a live flamingo as a mallet – both creatures having 'wills of their own'. But equally we could not play croquet if the balls moved like stars in their courses regardless of the players' wishes and plans.

I argued that the impetratory role of prayer requires large-scale two-way contingency in the observable world. But this is no difficulty against Christian belief if we have good reason to admit such contingency anyhow, as I have argued that we have. There are many large-scale future events in the physical world which are contingent in regard to all created causes, and which we cannot predict (even leaving aside the possibility of miracles) from consideration of any created causes; there has to be this element of chance in things if human choices are to have any *Spielraum* ['*scope*'], as they manifestly have. But such contingent events do not fall outside the order of Providence, which can arrange them so as to answer prayers. Whether and when the prayers are so answered, it is not for philosophy to say.

Peter Baelz, *Prayer and Providence: A Background Study*, London, SCM, 1968, pp. 16–21

In our own times no one has stressed the interdependence of belief and prayer more forcibly than Karl Barth, and I shall venture here to quote from him at some length. In his *Evangelical Theology*, he includes a chapter in which he discusses the intimate connexion between theology and prayer (ET London, Collins, 1965, pp. 148–58). According to him 'the first and basic act of theological work is prayer'. This is not intended as a polite formality, like the Latin grace before hall dinner, nor even as a brief petition for God's help in the pursuit of theological truth. It is something much more fundamental. 'Theological work does not merely begin with prayer and is not merely accompanied by it; in its totality it is peculiar and characteristic of theology that it can be performed only in the act of prayer.' No prayer, no theology!

Barth makes the following four points in elucidating his meaning. First, he refers to the peculiar epistemological status of the object of theological study. We cannot grasp it; it can only grasp us. That is, the proper object of theology, namely God, is not at our disposal, it is not a feature of our world which can be observed and pointed out in any detached manner.

. . .

Second, we cannot take it for granted that when we are using the word 'God' we are in fact talking about God. We need to be continually illuminated by the divine light. 'Proper and useful theological work is distinguished by the fact that it takes place in a realm which not only has open windows (which in themselves are admittedly good and necessary) facing the surrounding life of the Church and world, but also and above all has a skylight. That is to say, theological work is opened *by* heaven and God's work and word, but it is also open *towards* heaven and God's work and word. It cannot possibly be taken for granted that this work is performed in this *open* realm, open towards the object of theology, its source and goal.' Again, 'What theologian is there who is not continually surprised to find, even when he endeavours wholly and perhaps very seriously to press forward to relatively true and important insights and statements, that he is moving about in a human, all too human, circle like a squirrel in a cage?'

. . .

Third, 'the object of theological work is not some *thing* but some *one*. . . . And he, this One, exists not as an idle and mute being for himself, but precisely in this *work* which is also his *Word*'. If man wishes to know God, he must hear God's word; and if he is to hear, he must listen. 'The task of theological work consists in listening to him, this One who speaks through his work, and in rendering account of his Word to oneself, the Church, and the world. . . . For this reason all human thought and speech in relation to God can have only the character of a *response* to be made to God's word.'

. . .

Fourth, theology can never assume that there are assured results of past theological reflection on which it is possible to build with perfect confidence for the future. The theologian's 'only possible procedure every day, in fact every hour, is to begin anew at the beginning'. This derives from the fact that the theologian is dependent for the object of his study upon the free decision of that object, namely God, to make himself available. 'The ever-new start is the only possible way because the object of theology is the living God himself in his free grace. . . . Theological work cannot be done on any level or in any respect other than by freely granting the free God room to dispose at will over everything that men may already have known, produced, and achieved, and over all the religious, moral, intellectual, spiritual, or divine equipage with which men have travelled. . . . It is a fact that this work can be and is done with vigour only when it is done not in some sort of rearmament over against its object but in the undaunted disarmament and capitulation to its object – that is to say, in the work of prayer.'

What are we to make of this? It may seem to some that we have lingered too long in the Barthian hot-house. We may be puzzled by the radically personalistic language in which Barth speaks of man's relationship to God. How far, we ask, does such language reflect the ontological structure of this relationship, and how far the psychological temperament of those who have a particular kind of religious experience engendered by a particular style of preaching? Barth writes almost as if God confronted man and spoke to him in very much the same sort of way as the preacher confronts his congregation and speaks to them from the exalted height of the pulpit. . . . Again, we may wonder whether Barth's insistence on the radical freedom of God and on the consequent instability of the theological enterprise unless it is from moment to moment reconstituted by God's gracious self-disclosure does not suggest a God whose freedom borders upon an arbitrariness barely compatible with his wisdom and faithfulness. Despite these misgivings we may derive something of fundamental importance from Barth's exposition.

His use of personal categories and his emphasis on the freedom of God play an important part in our understanding both of the transcendence of God and of man's knowledge of God. It is characteristic of personal being at the human level that a man is not completely bound by his nature, that he has the freedom, limited though it clearly is, to transcend what the past has made him. Through this freedom he can exercise a certain creativity and claim a certain responsibility. He can give himself to other persons or he can withhold himself. Personal being, then, can provide us with an appropriate language with which to speak of the being of God. However, whereas man is bound to the world and only in a measure free, God is not bound to the world in a corresponding dependence. His freedom is absolute. The world is the object of God's creative activity but God does not, as man does, derive his being in any respect from the created world. The created world as such may disclose or it may conceal the presence of the creative God, but it discloses it only in so far as God chooses of his free grace to reveal himself. Thus the language of freedom and of personal relationship is used to reflect an ontological structure – to suggest a fundamental discontinuity between the being of God and the being of the world and at the same time to leave room for the possibility of man's coming to know God simply because God wills to make himself known. Prayer can then be seen as a serious attempt to prepare for God's gracious self-disclosure and faith as the acknowledgement of this self-disclosure, an acknowledgement which is itself an expression of prayer – 'My Lord and my God'.

Paul Helm, 'Prayer and Providence', in Gijsbert van den Brink, Luco van den Brom and Marcel Sarot (eds), *Christian Faith and Philosophical Theology*, **Kampen, The Netherlands, Kok Pharos, 1992, pp. 103–5, 109–15**

A major assumption made by Professor Brümmer throughout his study [*What Are We Doing When We Pray?*] is that personal relations, both inter-human and divine-human relations, must be free, understanding this in an indeterministic sense. If a relationship is to be truly personal both parties to it must contribute indeterministically free actions to it. One consequence which is drawn from this assumption is that since actions in an interpersonal situation are not governed by causal necessity, they cannot be manipulated by either party. So it is impossible for God to manipulate creaturely persons and, more importantly in our present context, impossible for those creaturely persons to manipulate God by, for example, praying to him. Such manipulative prayer would be a form of magic.

. . .

On these assumptions about personal relations the metaphysical side of Professor Brümmer's account of impetratory prayer is largely erected. Thus it follows from this view of personal relations that no account of God's power over and knowledge of human beings can be accepted which has deterministic implications. And because personal relations are necessarily *temporal* relations, that is they can only occur in a temporal sequence, an account of personal relations 'presupposes a God who can have a temporal relation with man and the world' (p. 42). And so God is in time.

. . .

In the light of this general argument I wish to offer a defence of Aquinas against the criticisms of Brümmer, and then to pose some difficulties for his own account.

Professor Brümmer considers the answer given by Thomas Aquinas to the relation between providence and prayer. Aquinas wrote:

> Divine providence not only disposes what effects will take place, but also the manner in which they will take place, and which actions will cause them. Human acts are true causes, and therefore men must perform certain actions, not in order to change divine providence, but in order to obtain certain effects in the manner determined by God. What is true of natural causes is true also of prayer, for we do not pray in order to change the decree of divine providence, rather we pray in order to acquire by petitionary prayer what God has determined would be obtained by our prayers. (*Summa Theologiae*, IIa IIae, 83, 2)

Brümmer poses two objections to this view. These are that the deterministic universe which Brümmer believes is implied by Aquinas' doctrine of an eternal divine decree excludes the impetratory character of petitionary prayer, and that on this view petitionary prayers are not impetratory at all. Brümmer asserts: 'They are the (eternally decreed) direct causes of the events prayed for and not requests to God to bring these events about' (p. 51). These two objections reduce to one: *No prayer can be truly impetratory if it is divinely-decreed.* The reason for this is the by-now familiar one that divinely-decreed events are determined, and no determined event can be an action that is constitutive of a genuinely personal relationship.

. . .

Suppose the following non-theological case. A promises to B that should he at any time need to borrow his ladders then all he needs to do is ask for them. This certainly looks like a case of a personal relation; indeed perhaps it is a case of a symmetrical personal relation: A and B, let us suppose, are friends and A's promise looks like a personal, intentional action. What the promise appears to do is to specify a sufficient condition for a request being granted; to obtain the ladders, all that B needs to do is ask and the ladders will be his.

What is true of this non-theological example would appear to be true of the parallel theological case. Suppose that God were to say: if you seek me you shall find me, understanding this as a promise and not as a mere prediction. If Jones seeks God then, assuming that God's promise holds good, Jones will find God; his seeking, given the promise, is a sufficient condition of his finding God.

Not only is this a possible sort of case but given what Scripture says about the place of divine promises in prayer, as well as the history of Christian piety, it is a sort of case that is central to an understanding of petitionary prayer. If this example is coherent then it cannot be the case that whatever is causally sufficient is manipulative, as Brümmer asserts.

. . .

For some prayers at least, for example those that are warranted by a promise, it is not necessary for the personal relation to be established that God is responsive and hence that God exists in time, as Brümmer claims (p. 42). For there is no *a priori* reason why the warrants should not be eternally established. That is, there is no reason why God should not timelessly decree the promise that if anyone seeks him then he will find him. And if this is so then for an important class of prayers it could be the case both that there is a personal relation between God and the one who prays and that God is timelessly eternal.

. . .

There is one little-examined moral implication of intercessory prayer based upon a causally-indeterminate view of human action. Such a view appears to place the whole of the burden of responsibility upon the one who intercedes (or who fails to intercede). For if a person genuinely believes that some particular evil is averted if and only if an intercessor properly intercedes for its removal, then the burden of responsibility for the continuing evil falls only and solely upon the shoulders of the intercessor. For the evil continues, on this view, only because the intercessor has not prayed sufficiently fervently, or sincerely, or at length, for the removal of the evil. So that it is valid to argue: If only A had prayed harder, X would have been averted.

Who is to blame for Auschwitz? On this view the blame at least for the continuation of the atrocity, once it has come to the notice of a potential intercessor, is not Nazi Germany, nor God, but the numerous potential intercessors who did not pray as hard or as sincerely as they might have done. Whether or not such a view is in accordance with Scripture and mainstream Christian belief is one thing. Another, more philosophical, but equally serious objection is that the burden of such failure upon us all would be insupportable.

Aquinas' view, cited by Professor Brümmer, whatever its other defects, does not have this problem for two reasons. One reason is that on this view prayer is a God-ordained means of fulfilling what God wills.

Intercessory prayer is not a means of settling God's mind on a course of action, but one of the ways in which the settled mind of God effects what he has decreed. So the 'burden of responsibility' for the answering or not answering of intercessory prayers, if one is permitted to use that expression, is placed firmly upon shoulders wide and strong enough to bear it. The intercession is fully integrated into the fulfilling of the divine decree. And so there is an inevitable tension, in intercessory prayer, between the need to integrate the will of the intercessor with the will of God, and the desire of the intercessor for certain changes in the universe which may, or may not, be in accordance with the divine will.

Secondly, on the view of Aquinas, as regards intercessory prayer the mind of God is not a *tabula rasa*, waiting to be imprinted with the wishes of the intercessors. It is already imprinted with his own will. The relation between an intercession and its answer or refusal is thus non-natural or conventional in character. To illustrate, let us suppose the existence of a powerful and benevolent agency. Two identical requests, say for a sum of money, are made to it. As far as I can see the only explanation of why one request was granted and the other refused which is open to someone who takes Professor Brümmer's view of intercession must be a natural one, due to the presence or absence of some hidden causal factor in the situation. On the view of Aquinas, the explanation lies in the will of the agency; it is not natural but conventional in character. Perhaps, for example, the agency had an agreement with one of the people making the request to make payment upon request, and had no such agreement with the other. Perhaps there was an obligation on the agency to make payment to the one and not the other.

To conclude, why does *any* prayer get answered? The answer to that question cannot be in terms of the benevolence of God, since that proves too much. If the reason why one prayer is answered is that God is benevolent then why are not all prayers answered? Nor can the answer be in terms of the strength of the intercessor since that places an insupportable burden on those intercessions which fail through weakness, or which are never made. The answer must, therefore, be not natural but conventional, in terms of the structure of will and warrant disclosed by God: only if A prayed in accordance with the divine will thus disclosed would his prayer be answered.

3.5 Prayer and the will of God

Friedrich Schleiermacher, 'The Power of Prayer in Relation to Outward Circumstances', from *Selected Sermons*, ET London, Hodder & Stoughton, 1890 (reprinted in Keith Clements (ed.), *Friedrich Schleiermacher: Pioneer of Modern Theology*, ET London, Collins, 1987, pp. 188–9)

Let us see then . . . what really is the effect of our prayers, if it is not to be sought in the agreement of the result with the expressed wish. Just the effect that it produced in Christ's own case. . . . He began with the definite wish that his sufferings might pass away from him; but as soon as he fixed his thought on his father in heaven to whom he prayed, this wish was at once qualified by the humble 'if it be possible'. When from the sleeping disciples, the sight of whom must have still more disheartened him and added fresh bitterness to his sense of desertion, he returned to prayer, he already bent his own wish before the thought that the will of the Father might be something different. To reconcile himself to this, and willingly to consent to it, was now his chief object; nor would he have wished that the will of God should not be done, had he been able by that means to gain all the world could give.

And when he had prayed for the third time all anxiety and dread were gone. He had no longer any wish of his own. With words in which he sought to impart to them some of the courage he had gained, he awakened his friends from their sleep, and went with calm spirit and holy firmness to meet the traitor.

There you see the effect that such a prayer ought to have. It should make us cease from our eager longing for the possession of some earthly good, or the averting of some dreaded evil; it should bring us courage to want, or to suffer, if God has so appointed it; it should lift us up out of the helplessness into which we are brought by fear and passion, and bring us to the consciousness and full use of our powers; that so we may be able in all circumstances to conduct ourselves as it becomes those who remember that they are living and acting under the eye and the protection of the most high.

Ian T. Ramsey, *Our Understanding of Prayer*, London, SPCK, 1971, pp. 17–18

If what we have prayed for (for example, the recovery of a friend from a serious illness) does not occur, let us be careful lest we say that what we had desired was 'not God's will', for this may seem to carry the implication that God has deliberately, with a particular intention, caused the friend's death. We should rather conclude that on this occasion we have not envisaged God's activity aright: we have not in our prayers portrayed a situation in harmony with the broad activity of God. In this context we can see why in one sense the first and last prayer will be 'Thy will be done'. For that faith, when rightly understood, is in no way expressive of a hopeless resignation. It is rather expressive of a hoped-for harmony between, on the one hand, the pattern of life we have explicated in our prayers and, on the other hand, the activity of God, which we know in response. If that hoped-for harmony does not materialize, the phrase is a reminder to us that in the last resort the aim of all prayer is for harmony between our activity and the activity of God which confronts us.

When Jesus was in Gethsemane (Mark 14 and parallels) he prayed 'that, if it were possible, the hour might pass from him' (v. 35). In other words, he brought a situation before God in the hope that the direction of his own will might harmonise with that of God. There could only be one aim – harmonious activity: 'Nevertheless, not what I will, but what thou wilt' (v. 36). So with ourselves, the phrase from Whittier's hymn expresses the intention of all prayer: 'All as God wills . . . ?' Our hope is that in and through our prayers we shall discern a providence of love expressing itself actively through all the events of our lives, and creating a pattern whose character becomes clearer over the passage of the years. It is this broad providential discernment, nothing more nor less than this, which is the ultimate hope of prayer. Prayer witnesses to a love, to which we respond in love. Prayer then will always aim to create a pattern which can be a symbol of, and through which can be expressed, a harmonious, loving co-operation between God and ourselves.

D. Z. Phillips, *The Concept of Prayer*, London, Routledge and Kegan Paul, 1965, pp. 117–21

The question, 'Why did this happen?' is asked, more often than not, in face of tragedy: the death of a child or early bereavement in marriage, for example. 'Why was my son taken?' a mother asks. This seems to imply that her son might not have been taken, and that God had good reason for taking him. Mothers often ask in such circumstances, 'Didn't I pray hard enough?' The suggestion is that if she had prayed hard enough her son would not have died. Sometimes, the question 'Why?' in these contexts is simply an expression of bewilderment. Or again, 'Didn't I pray hard enough?' might mean that the mother thought she had some measure of blame in the matter. Given, however, that the mother *does* believe that increased prayer would have saved her son, one must say that the prayer is superstition. In the superstitious sense, 'I didn't pray hard enough' is akin to, 'The spell was not powerful enough'. Prayer seems to be conceived of as acting on God in some way. We have already rejected the analogy between prayer and incantation. A similar explanation can be given of the prayer of someone who prays in a storm, 'O God, don't let the lightning hit my house'. Sometimes, this almost seems to mean, 'Let the lightning hit someone else's house'! What is one to say about this kind of prayer? One can say that one does not like it, but that is neither here nor there. The prayer reveals the attitude of the person concerned to the way things go. It reveals little devotion, since if the house were hit, one could imagine the event resulting in a loss of faith. It is probable that the prayer is thought of as an attempt to influence God's directing of the lightning. If this is true, the prayer is superstition and nothing else.

. . .

An objection might be made against drawing a rigid distinction between prayers and effective spells by drawing attention to prayers of petition, and prayers which give thanks for answers to such petitions. There is a suggestion here that the prayer has been effective in some way or other. What of parents who pray for a dying child, 'O God, don't let her die!'? If the prayer is not to be regarded as superstition, it cannot be thought of as an attempt to *influence* God to heal the child. But what of the instances where the prayer has been answered? Does not the answer show that God has answered the petition? Certainly, but the *philosophical* question is about what it *means* to say that God has answered the petition. What then does it mean when parents pray after the child's recovery, 'We thank Thee for her recovery'? It might be suggested that one cannot understand the thanksgiving unless one admits that God might not have spared the child. This is true: *the child might have died*. Parents pray for their children to be spared, but they still die. Is one to say that God has good reasons for saving some children but not others? We have already seen the consequences of doing so. Or are we to lay the blame, for that is what we are doing when we talk like this, at the door of the parents, and say that they did not pray as hard as other parents? Obviously, it is extremely misleading and dangerous to pursue this line of argument. But how does one reconcile these prayers of petition with the idea of the will of God and thanking God for one's existence, in which I have claimed that the grammar of the language of prayer can be found?

. . .

Medical treatment has failed, and a child is dying. Religious parents pray, 'O God, let her live'. What does this amount to? The parents recognize that things can go either way; the child may live or it may die. Indeed, in this case, it looks as if the child will die. But they meet the possibility of things going either way in God. They recognize their own helplessness, that the way things go is beyond their control, and seek something to sustain them which does not depend on the way things go, namely, the love of God. If the child recovers, the recovery *occasions* the prayer of thanksgiving. If one thinks in terms of causing God to save the child, one is nearer the example of non-religious parents who pray, 'O God, save our child' where the thought behind the prayer is that God could save the child if he wanted to. The prayer is an attempt at influencing the divine will. In short, one is back in the realm of superstition. It is true that love of God's will can be found in whatever happens, but the prayer of petition is best understood, not as an attempt at influencing the way things go, but as an expression of, and a request for, devotion to God through the way things go.

. . .

What I want to say of petitionary prayers is analogous to what I said of prayers of confession. When deep religious believers pray *for* something, they are not so much asking God to bring this about, but in a way telling him of the strength of their desires. They realize that things may not go as they wish, but they are asking to be able to go on living whatever happens. In prayers of confession and in prayers of petition, the believer is trying to find a meaning and a hope that will deliver him from the elements in his life which threaten to destroy it: in the first case, his guilt, and in the second case, his desires.

3.6 Prayer and work

Geoffrey Wainwright, *Doxology: The Praise of God in Worship, Doctrine and Life*, London, Epworth, 1980, pp. 24–6

> Blessed are you, Lord, God of all creation. Through your goodness we have this bread to offer, which earth has given and human hands have made. It will become for us the bread of life.

Blessed are you, Lord, God of all creation. Through your goodness we have this wine to offer, fruit of the vine and work of human hands. It will become our spiritual drink.

. . .

The prayers just quoted from the Roman Missal mention the part played by human labour in the process by which the material creation becomes the means of communion with God. Work is thus taken up into prayer; it becomes the stuff of prayer. Conversely, the attitude of prayer should inform our daily work. In the words of George Herbert which figure in many hymn-books:

> Teach me, my God and King,
>   In all things Thee to see;
> And what I do in anything,
>   To do it as for Thee.

. . .

> A servant with this clause
>   Makes drudgery divine;
> Who sweeps a room, as for Thy laws,
>   Makes that and the action fine.

> This is the famous stone
>   That turneth all to gold:
> For that which God doth touch and own,
>   Cannot for less be told.

In this way, the adage becomes true: *laborare est orare*, to work is to pray.

It is Christian experience, however, that the adage can also be reversed: to pray is to work. The Hebrew word '*abad* (to serve) is used for both work and worship. Our word 'liturgy' contains the Greek *ergon* (work). The early Fathers called prayer a *kopos*, a hard task. Work is energy directed towards a goal. The offering of ourselves in worship is the active direction of our whole personal being towards God.

Topics for discussion

1 What is the primary point of prayer?
2 Are there any attitudes that are incompatible with prayer (fear, doubt, anger with God, desire for revenge)?
3 How should we conceive of God answering prayer? Has he already taken our prayers into account as part of his providential plan (Aquinas, Lewis, Helm), or is the world sufficiently open for us to think in terms of his making a direct personal response (Geach, Brümmer)? What would Phillips say?
4 Is Helm right that the personal response account of prayer would place too heavy a moral burden on us to pray? Or are the results of intercessory prayer unfair whatever answer is given to question 3?
5 How plausible are naturalistic accounts of prayer, such as auto-suggestion (for petitionary prayer), telepathy and resonance (for intercessory prayer)? Need they necessarily be seen as *opposed to* a religious explanation?
6 Is Barth correct about the close dependency of theology upon prayer? Does his view imply that a non-Christian would have nothing to contribute? What is your position here?
7 Give a theological assessment of D. Z. Phillips' account of petitionary prayer.
8 '*Laborare est orare*' (Ecclesiasticus 38:34). Is the Benedictine ideal of the complete integration of prayer and work a worthy goal, or does it confuse two very different kinds of activity?

4   Grace

4.1 Grace in the Bible

Deuteronomy 8:12–18, 9:5–6

8 [12]When you have eaten your fill and have built fine houses and live in them, [13]and when your herds and flocks have multiplied, and your silver and gold is multiplied, and all that you have is multiplied, [14]then do not exalt yourself, forgetting the LORD your God, who brought you out of the land of Egypt, out of the house of slavery, [15]who led you through the great and terrible wilderness, an arid waste-land with poisonous snakes and scorpions. He made water flow for you from flint rock, [16]and fed you in the wilderness with manna that your ancestors did not know, to humble you and to test you, and in the end to do you good. [17]Do not say to yourself, 'My power and the might of my own hand have gained me this wealth.' [18]But remember the LORD your God, for it is he who gives you power to get wealth, so that he may confirm his covenant that he swore to your ancestors, as he is doing today.

. . .

9 [5]It is not because of your righteousness or the uprightness of your heart that you are going in to occupy their land; but because of the wickedness of those nations that the LORD your God is dispossessing them before you, in order to fulfil the promise that the LORD made on oath to your ancestors, to Abraham, to Isaac, and to Jacob.

[6] Know, then, that the LORD your God is not giving you this good land to occupy because of your righteousness; for you are a stubborn people.

Psalm 136:1, 23–6

1 O give thanks to the Lord, for he is
    good,
      for his steadfast love endures for
      ever.

         . . .

23 It is he who remembered us in our
    low estate,
      for his steadfast love endures for
      ever;
24 and rescued us from our foes,
      for his steadfast love endures for
      ever;
25 who gives food to all flesh,
      for his steadfast love endures for
      ever.
26 O give thanks to the God of heaven,
      for his steadfast love endures for
      ever.

Isaiah 43:2–3a, 14–15

43 2When you pass through the waters, I
      will be with you;
  and through the rivers, they shall
    not overwhelm you;
when you walk through fire you shall
    not be burned,
  and the flame shall not
    consume you.
3 For I am the Lord your God,
    the Holy One of Israel, your
    Saviour.

         . . .

14 Thus says the Lord,
    your Redeemer, the Holy One
      of Israel:

> For your sake I will send to Babylon
> and break down all the bars,
> and the shouting of the Chaldeans
> will be turned to lamentation.
> 15 I am the LORD, your Holy One,
> the Creator of Israel, your King.

Romans 3:21–6, 5:1–17

3 [21]But now, irrespective of law, the righteousness of God has been disclosed, and is attested by the law and the prophets, [22]the righteousness of God through faith in Jesus Christ for all who believe. For there is no distinction, [23]since all have sinned and fall short of the glory of God; [24]they are now justified by his grace as a gift, through the redemption that is in Christ Jesus, [25]whom God put forward as a sacrifice of atonement by his blood, effective through faith. He did this to show his righteousness, because in his divine forbearance he had passed over the sins previously committed; [26]it was to prove at the present time that he himself is righteous and that he justifies the one who has faith in Jesus.

. . .

5 [1]Therefore, since we are justified by faith, we have peace with God through our Lord Jesus Christ, [2]through whom we have obtained access to this grace in which we stand; and we boast in our hope of sharing the glory of God.

. . .

[6]For while we were still weak, at the right time Christ died for the ungodly. [7]Indeed, rarely will anyone die for a righteous person – though perhaps for a good person someone might actually dare to die. [8]But God proves his love for us in that while we still were sinners Christ died for us. [9]Much more surely then, now that we have been justified by his blood, will we be saved through him from the wrath of God. [10]For if while we were enemies, we were reconciled to God through the death of his Son, much more surely, having been reconciled, will we be saved by his life. [11]But more than that, we even boast in God through our Lord Jesus Christ, through whom we have now received reconciliation.

[12]Therefore, just as sin came into the world through one man, and death came through sin, and so death spread to all because all have sinned – [13]sin was indeed in the world before the law, but sin is not reckoned when there is no law. [14]Yet death exercised dominion from

Adam to Moses, even over those whose sins were not like the transgression of Adam, who is a type of the one who was to come.

¹⁵But the free gift is not like the trespass. For if the many died through the one man's trespass, much more surely have the grace of God and the free gift in the grace of the one man, Jesus Christ, abounded for the many. ¹⁶And the free gift is not like the effect of the one man's sin. For the judgement following one trespass brought condemnation, but the free gift following many trespasses brings justification. ¹⁷If, because of the one man's trespass, death exercised dominion through that one, much more surely will those who receive the abundance of grace and the free gift of righteousness exercise dominion in life through the one man, Jesus Christ.

Ephesians 2:1–10

2 ¹You were dead through the trespasses and sins ²in which you once lived, following the course of this world, following the ruler of the power of the air, the spirit that is now at work among those who are disobedient. ³All of us once lived among them in the passions of our flesh, following the desires of flesh and senses, and we were by nature children of wrath, like everyone else. ⁴But God, who is rich in mercy, out of the great love with which he loved us ⁵even when we were dead through our trespasses, made us alive together with Christ – by grace you have been saved – ⁶and raised us up with him and seated us with him in the heavenly places in Christ Jesus, ⁷so that in the ages to come he might show the immeasurable riches of his grace in kindness towards us in Christ Jesus. ⁸For by grace you have been saved through faith, and this is not your own doing; it is the gift of God – ⁹not the result of works, so that no one may boast. ¹⁰For we are what he has made us, created in Christ Jesus for good works, which God prepared beforehand to be our way of life.

John 1:14–17

1 ¹⁴And the Word became flesh and lived among us, and we have seen his glory, the glory as of a father's only son, full of grace and truth. ¹⁵(John testified to him and cried out, 'This was he of whom I said, "He who comes after me ranks ahead of me because he was before me." ') ¹⁶From his fullness we have all received, grace upon grace. ¹⁷The law indeed was given through Moses; grace and truth came through Jesus Christ.

4.2 Augustine on grace and freedom

Augustine, *On Nature and Grace*, III.3–IV.4

Human nature was at the very beginning created without blame or any fault. That nature with which anyone from Adam is born is now in need of a doctor because it is not healthy. All the good things which it has in its formation, life, senses and mind, it has from the supreme God, its creator and designer. But the fault which darkens and weakens those natural goods, with the result that it has need of enlightening and healing, has not been acquired from a guiltless designer, but comes from original sin which was perpetrated by free will. On this account human nature is liable to punishment and to a most just retribution. For, if we are now in Christ a new creature (cf. 2 Corinthians 5:17), yet by nature we are children of wrath, just like the rest of humanity. But God who is rich in mercy, on account of the great love with which he loved us even when we were dead in our sins, has brought us again to life with Christ, by whose grace we are saved (cf. Ephesians 2:3 – 5).

But this grace of Christ, without which neither children nor those of mature age can be saved, is not a return for merit but given without prior conditions (*gratis*), for which reason it is indeed called grace (*gratia*). We are justified, he says, through his blood. Accordingly, it is those who are not freed by that blood (whether because they have not yet been able to hear, or been unwilling to obey, or even not been able to hear on account of their youth, and so have not received the regenerating bath which they could receive and through which they might have been saved) who are justly condemned in any case because they are not without sin, whether they have derived this from their human origins or because they have added to it by evil practices. For all have sinned, whether in Adam or in themselves, and fallen short of the glory of God (cf. Romans 3:23).

Augustine, *On the Spirit and Letter*, III.5

We say that the human will is so aided by God towards the doing of righteousness (*iustitia*) that apart from the fact that humanity is created with free choice of will and given teaching by which it is instructed in the manner in which it ought to live, it also receives the Holy Spirit by whom there is formed in its own mind a delight and love of that supreme and unchangeable good which is God. This is even now taking place while we still walk through faith and not yet by sight (cf. 2 Corinthians 5:7). The result is that, with this pledge as it were of a free gift given to itself (cf. 2 Corinthians 5:5), the human being is aflame with desire to cling to its creator, and burns to draw close to participate in that true light, so that it may derive its flourishing from him from whom it already has its being. For, if the way of truth is hidden, free will does not have any strength whatever except in leading to sin. But even when what must be done and striven for has begun no more to lie hidden, unless there is delight and love, it will not be done nor undertaken nor bring living well. In order to love, the love of God is poured into our hearts, not through free will which arises from within ourselves but through the Holy Spirit which is given to us (cf. Romans 5:5).

Pelagius, as reported by Augustine in his *On the Grace of Christ and Original Sin*, IV.5

We distinguish three things, and separate and assign them as it were into a certain order. In the first place we put possibility (*posse*), in the second willing (*velle*) and in the third being (*esse*). Possibility we place in the realm of nature, willing in the will, and being in the sphere of what actually happens. The first of these, that is, possibility, properly pertains to God who has assigned it to his creatures; the two remaining, that is, willing and being, should be referred to humanity itself, since they originate from their source in the will. Therefore, praise for human beings lies in the will and in good action; or rather both to human beings and to God because it is God who gives the possibility of the willing itself and of the resultant action, who himself always aids that possibility with the help of his own grace. The fact that a human being can will the good and accomplish it is due to God alone. . . . Wherefore (what must often be repeated because of your false accusations) when we say that it is possible for human beings to be without sin, we are praising God also by acknowledgment of that possibility, a God who has bestowed precisely that possibility on us, nor is there any occasion for praising human beings where the cause is a matter of God alone. For it is not a question of willing or being but solely of what is possible.

4.3 Locating grace

Dietrich Bonhoeffer, *The Cost of Discipleship*, ET London, SCM, 1959, pp. 35–7

Cheap grace is the deadly enemy of our Church. We are fighting to-day for costly grace.

Cheap grace means grace sold on the market like cheapjack's wares. The sacraments, the forgiveness of sin, and the consolations of religion are thrown away at cut prices. Grace is represented as the Church's inexhaustible treasury, from which she showers blessings with generous hands, without asking questions or fixing limits. Grace without price; grace without cost! The essence of grace, we suppose, is that the account has been paid in advance; and, because it has been paid, everything can be had for nothing. Since the cost was infinite, the possibilities of using and spending it are infinite. What would grace be if it were not cheap?

. . .

Cheap grace means the justification of sin without the justification of the sinner. Grace alone does everything, they say, and so everything can remain as it was before. 'All for sin could not atone.' The world goes on in the same old way, and we are still sinners 'even in the best life' as Luther said. Well, then, let the Christian live like the rest of the world, let him model himself on the world's standards in every sphere of life, and not presumptuously aspire to live a different life under grace from his old life under sin.

. . .

Instead of following Christ, let the Christian enjoy the consolations of his grace! That is what we mean by cheap grace, the grace which amounts to the justification of sin without the justification of the repentant sinner who departs from sin and from whom sin departs. Cheap grace is not the kind of forgiveness of sin which frees us from the toils of sin. Cheap grace is the grace we bestow on ourselves.

Cheap grace is the preaching of forgiveness without requiring repentance, baptism without church discipline, Communion without confession, absolution without personal confession. Cheap grace is grace without discipleship, grace without the cross, grace without Jesus Christ, living and incarnate.

Costly grace is the treasure hidden in the field; for the sake of it a man will gladly go and sell all that he has. It is the pearl of great price to buy which the merchant will sell all his goods. It is the kingly rule of Christ, for whose sake a man will pluck out the eye which causes him to stumble, it is the call of Jesus Christ at which the disciple leaves his nets and follows him.

Costly grace is the gospel which must be *sought* again and again, the gift which must be *asked* for, the door at which a man must *knock*.

Such grace is *costly* because it calls us to follow, and it is *grace* because it calls us to follow *Jesus Christ*. It is costly because it costs a man his life, and it is grace because it gives a man the only true life. It is costly because it condemns sin, and grace because it justifies the sinner. Above all, it is *costly* because it cost God the life of his Son: 'ye were bought at a price' [*1 Corinthians 7:23*], and what has cost God much cannot be cheap for us. Above all, it is *grace* because God did not reckon his Son too dear a price to pay for our life, but delivered him up for us. Costly grace is the Incarnation of God. . . . Grace is costly because it compels a man to submit to the yoke of Christ and follow him; it is grace because Jesus says: 'My yoke is easy and my burden is light' [*Matthew 11:30*].

Karl Rahner, *Theological Investigations*, Vol. III, ET London, Darton, Longman and Todd, 1967, pp. 86–9

Have we ever actually experienced grace? We do not mean by this some pious feeling, a sort of festive religious uplift, or any soft comfort, but precisely the experiencing of grace, i.e. of that visitation by the Holy Spirit of the triune God which has become a reality in Christ through his becoming man and through his sacrifice on the Cross. Is it possible at all to experience grace in this life? Would not an affirmative answer to this question mean the destruction of faith, of that semi-obscure cloud which envelops us as long as we are pilgrims on this earth? The mystics do indeed tell us – and they would testify to the truth of their assertion by laying down their lives – that they have already experienced God and hence also grace. But this empirical knowledge of God in mystic experience is an obscure and mysterious matter about which one cannot speak if one has not experienced it, and about which one will not speak if one has. Our question, therefore, cannot be answered simply *a priori*. But perhaps there are steps in the experience of grace, the lowest of which is accessible even to us?

Let us ask ourselves to begin with: have we ever experienced the *spiritual* in man? (What is meant here by spirit is itself a difficult question which cannot be answered simply and in a few words.) We will perhaps answer: of course, I have experienced this and in fact experience it every day. I think, I study, I make decisions, I act, I enter into relationships with others, I live in a community which is based not only on biological but also on spiritual factors, I love, I am happy, I enjoy poetry, I possess cultural, scientific, artistic values, etc. In short, I know what spirit is. Yet it is not quite as simple as that. Everything we have stated is perfectly true.

But in all these things the 'spirit' is (or can be) merely, as it were, the ingredient which is used for making this earthly life human, beautiful and in some way meaningful. Yet it does not follow that we have thereby already experienced the spirit in its proper transcendence. This does not mean, of course, that spirit as such is to be found only where one speaks and philosophizes about the transcendence of the spirit. Quite the contrary: that would merely be a derived and secondary experience of that spirit which does not govern the life of man merely as one of its inner moments. Where then lies the real experience? At this point we would like to say from the very start: let us try to discover it for ourselves in our experience; and to aid this, one can merely tentatively and cautiously point out certain things.

Have we ever kept quiet, even though we wanted to defend ourselves when we had been unfairly treated? Have we ever forgiven someone even though we got no thanks for it and our silent forgiveness was taken for granted? Have we ever obeyed, not because we had to and because otherwise things would have become unpleasant for us, but simply on account of that mysterious, silent, incomprehensible being we call God and his will? Have we ever sacrificed something without receiving any thanks or recognition for it, and even without a feeling of inner satisfaction? Have we ever been absolutely lonely? Have we ever decided on some course of action purely by the innermost judgement of our conscience, deep down where one can no longer tell or explain it to anyone, where one is quite alone and knows that one is taking a decision which no one else can take in one's place and for which one will have to answer for all eternity? Have we ever tried to love God when we are no longer being borne on the crest of the wave of enthusiastic feeling, when it is no longer possible to mistake our self, and its vital urges, for God? Have we ever tried to love him when we thought we were dying of this love and when it seemed like death and absolute negation? Have we ever tried to love God when we seemed to be calling out into emptiness and our cry seemed to fall on deaf ears, when it looked as if we were taking a terrifying jump into the bottomless abyss, when everything seemed to become incomprehensible and apparently senseless? Have we ever fulfilled a duty when it seemed that it could be done only with a consuming sense of really betraying and obliterating oneself, when it could apparently be done only by doing something terribly stupid for which no one would thank us? Have we ever been good to someone who did not show the slightest sign of gratitude or comprehension and when we also were not rewarded by the feeling of having been 'selfless', decent, etc.?

Let us search for ourselves in such experiences in our life; let us look for our own experiences in which things like this have happened to us individually. If we find such experiences, then we have experienced the spirit in the way meant here. For the experience meant here is the experience of eternity; it is the experience that the spirit is more than merely a part of this temporal world; the experience that man's meaning is not exhausted by the meaning and fortune of this world; the experience of the adventure and confidence of taking the plunge, an experience which no longer has any reason which can be demonstrated or which is taken from the success of this world.

. . .

To proceed: once we experience the spirit in this way, we (at least, we as Christians who live in faith) have also already *in fact* experienced the *supernatural*. We have done so perhaps in a very anonymous and inexpressible manner. Probably we have experienced it in such a way even that we were unable to turn round – and did not dare to do so – to look the supernatural straight in the face. But we know – when we let ourselves go in this experience of the spirit, when the tangible and assignable, the relishable element disappears, when everything takes on the taste of death and destruction, or when everything disappears as if in an inexpressible, as it were white, colourless and intangible beatitude – then in actual fact it is not merely the spirit but the Holy Spirit who is at work in us. Then is the hour of his grace. Then the seemingly uncanny, bottomless depth of our existence as experienced by us is the bottomless depth of God communicating himself to us, the dawning of his approaching infinity which no longer has any set paths, which is tasted like a nothing because it is infinity. When we have let ourselves go and no longer belong to ourselves, when we have denied ourselves and no longer have the disposing of ourselves, when everything (including ourselves) has moved away from us as if into an infinite distance, then we begin to live in the world of God himself, the world of the God of grace and of eternal life. This may still appear strange to us at the beginning, and we will always be tempted again to take fright and flee back into what is familiar and near to us: in fact, we will often have to and will often be allowed to do this. But we should gradually try to get ourselves used to the taste of the pure wine of the spirit, which is filled with the Holy Spirit. We should do this at least to the extent of not refusing the chalice when his directing providence offers it to us.

The chalice of the Holy Spirit is identical in this life with the chalice of

Christ. This chalice is drunk only by those who have slowly learned in little ways to taste the fullness in emptiness, the ascent in the fall, life in death, the finding in renunciation. Anyone who learns this, experiences the spirit – the pure spirit – and in this experience he is also given the experience of the Holy Spirit of grace. For this liberation of the spirit is attained on the whole and in the long run only by the grace of Christ in faith. Where he liberates this spirit, however, he liberates it by supernatural grace which introduces the spirit into the life of God himself.

Basil Mitchell, 'The Grace of God', in Mitchell (ed.), *Faith and Logic: Oxford Essays in Philosophical Theology*, London, George Allen & Unwin, 1957, pp. 161–2, 174–5

If the doctrine of grace is not open to scientific test and yet, as has been argued, is not without factual content, it remains to show how it can meet the logician's legitimate demand. What evidence can be called in support of it? If, as has been admitted, it does not function like an ordinary causal explanation, how *does* it function?

It was asserted at the beginning of this essay that belief in God's grace follows from belief in him as the creator of free persons. It is a necessary development from the Christian doctrine of God. Hence whatever evidences (if that word is at all appropriate) can be found to support that doctrine will go to support this too. But it was also suggested that there was independent support for the doctrine of grace in the religious experience of individuals and communities; but not *entirely* independent, because that experience is interpreted in terms of a religious tradition, based in its turn on the inspired scriptures. The argument has a circular motion, but this is not vicious, because each revolution brings in new material.

. . .

[T]here are two kinds of experience which invite interpretation in these terms, the impression of holiness made by the saint and the sense of a liberating power at work in oneself. The appeal to such things forms part of the familiar 'argument from religious experience'. It is an argument which is hard to state in a way which is at all convincing and hence is treated by philosophers and theologians with reserve. Yet such is the impact of the experiences themselves that it is never finally abandoned.

. . .

Belief in the grace of God cannot be established by empirical evidence but, once accepted, it can be seen to have empirical application.

But there is danger of a certain unbalance in approaching the doctrine from the empirical end. Challenged to defend the factual character of statements about grace by pointing to cases where it makes a detectable difference, we have been led to emphasize its more remarkable and striking manifestations. And this may easily convey the impression that grace has to do only with abnormal, *spectacular* irruptions into the lives of the professedly religious. This is one more reason why the argument from religious experience has not appealed to many sensitively religious minds. But a more broadly theological approach teaches us that we cannot presume to limit the divine activity to those instances in which it may be discernible to us. Such instances may be clearly revelatory (must be, if our previous argument is to have any force) yet they are revelatory of the God, whose activity we believe on general grounds, to underlie even the most tentative and inarticulate movements of the human soul towards conformity with the pattern of Christ. They are like the phosphorescent crest of a wave which enables us to detect a sea whose boundaries we could not chart. Having made an entry for the concept of grace by tracing it as it breaks through more or less spectacularly into human experience, we are led to extend its application to all good works, whether characterized by the numinous [*awe-inspiring*] or not, whether or not associated with religious belief. It is enough that they tend in the direction of that complete holiness, which is the 'fruit of the spirit'.

What secret workings of the human soul *do* tend in this direction, we are for the most part unable to say. We are rarely in a position to chart any man's spiritual history. Hence together with the conviction that in such conspicuous instances as the labours of St Paul the grace of God is clearly at work goes a marked hesitation to deny outright the activity of God even in the most unpromising events. (Though the word 'grace' itself is, perhaps, limited by definition to God's activity in and through the human person, *in so far as it is expressive of his nature*.)

David Brown, 'Butler and Deism', in Christopher Cunliffe (ed.),
Joseph Butler's Moral and Religious Thought: Tercentenary Essays,
Oxford, Oxford University Press, 1992, pp. 24–7

It is not clear that even God could successfully communicate what was radically at variance with what was already believed. For the only means of assessing a proposed new belief is our existing canons of judgement, and so any new belief to be intelligible has to be such as to be capable of being accommodated within those canons. That is to suggest that changes in belief occur gradually, with existing patterns of thought exercising a considerable restraining influence; but this seems confirmed by the history of thought. As philosophers are increasingly recognizing, even reason itself is not immune from the fact of historical conditioning. Models of rationality vary from century to century, and are often affected by hidden influences of which even outstanding intellects may be only partially aware.

But now, it may be objected, I have proved my point too well. For, if all thought, including the canons of reason, is historically conditioned, what grounds could there be for identifying an additional causal factor in the form of divine revelation? Such indeed is the line of attack which contemporary deism takes. Whereas in the eighteenth century the appeal was to canons of reason which transcended particular historical circumstance, in the twentieth the very fact of historical conditioning is used to undermine any claim that the means of access to knowledge could be fundamentally different from one generation to another. The result is that not only is miracle excluded but the insights of Scripture become merely a powerful expression of what was potentially available to us all.

In replacing the rationalist critique with an historicizing one Ernst Troeltsch played a leading role. His claim is that there are three main criteria with which the historical method operates, and that all three must inevitably rule out of court any theology which appeals to miracle or assigns a specific causal role to the supernatural. The three are: criticism (by which he means that historical judgements are always subject to revision and so never get beyond the status of assessments of probability); analogy (the need to assess such probability by comparison with our own experience and what we know to have happened elsewhere); and correlation (the assumption that events are intelligible only in so far as they can be shown to be part of an already existing causal pattern).

. . .

Troeltsch closes off a specific causal role for the supernatural on the grounds that the world we now encounter leaves no room for such a role, and so by analogy other cultures must have been similarly placed, however differently they may have expressed themselves. But it is arguable that he has misread the character of our world and that by taking seriously an alternative analogy a very different picture emerges, one in which a divine causal role once again becomes a serious possibility. This is the analogy between our own personal action and divine action.

However tight causal laws are at the inanimate level, most of us continue to believe in the fact of human freedom: that, though much may incline us to act in a particular way, under normal circumstances nothing forces us to do so. One way of making sense of this belief is to think that once a certain level of complexity is reached such as the human brain, the causal processes cease to operate entirely in one direction, from below to above, but that initiative becomes possible, with causal processes operating from above to below, and that is what we mean by the relative independence of the mind: without a brain the human mind cannot operate, but this does not preclude the mind controlling the operations of that brain. If that is so, it also becomes possible to understand how free human communication takes place. At one level it is all a matter of normal causal processes, the reception of sound and so forth, but at another it involves free human decision. Address and response are results of the human will, even though the means of communication are entirely determined by causal laws and indeed even the decision to communicate or respond may be heavily conditioned by the individual's historical circumstances. (To 'condition', however extreme, is not of course to 'determine'. There remains some room for manoeuvre on the part of the individual, however small.)

So, then, with God. To assert that God is personal must be to claim that there is at least as much room for manoeuvre for him in his dialogue with us as there is in normal human intercourse. Just as we can initiate an address to another human being without that address being caused, so similarly can God. Again, for that address to be heard various causal processes must operate, but once more there is no reason to think the situation any different with respect to God. For he too may be envisaged as normally operating through the usual causal processes. Occasionally, no doubt, visions and similar phenomena occur, but there is no reason to think this the normal pattern of divine interchange with human beings. Instead we may think of ideas apparently spontaneously occurring in our subconscious that really have their origin in divine action. Nor is that to speak of miracle, any more than is the appearance of such thoughts when they are produced by our own mind acting upon our brain. Then, what we make of these divinely given 'thoughts' will be partly up to us and our free decision, and partly a matter of the particular historical circumstances in which we find ourselves and the degree of cultural conditioning which these have exercised upon us.

With that as our model of the way in which grace can operate in our own lives, of the way in which God can interact with human beings in the present, it then becomes much easier to answer Troeltsch. For applying this analogy between human and divine communication to biblical revelation, we may say that the latter differs only in degree and not in kind from what we experience in our own lives. His objections on grounds of analogy and correlation are thus misplaced. The problem of correlation is answered because divine action is to be placed in the wider context of other kinds of personal action, not simply the unbroken system of cause and effect which pertains at the sub-personal level. Similarly the problem of analogy is answered because the activity of the biblical God is directly paralleled to the activity of God today, which in turn is paralleled by our own activity as personal agents. To object that what I have said thus far ignores the question of miracle would be to miss my point; for it is precisely my contention that to make the notion of revelation credible there is no need to resort to miracle. That is a distinct issue.

4.4 Personal or impersonal?

Stewart R. Sutherland, 'God and Freedom', in Colin E. Gunton (ed.), *God and Freedom: Essays in Historical and Systematic Theology,* **Edinburgh, T & T Clark, 1995, pp. 24, 27–9**

In the sixteenth century, a man called John Bradford, watching criminals being led to execution, uttered the often misquoted words: 'But for the grace of God, there goes John Bradford.'

. . .

[E]ach variation in the possible account which we might give of grace will lie on a spectrum between two limiting cases. At one end of the spectrum, the account given of the rôle of grace in the world of human purpose and action will differ little from talk of an impersonal working out of fortune, whether outrageous or not, which differs little from what we have been referring to as 'moral luck'. Thus: But for the absence of outrageous fortune, there goes John Bradford. In that extreme and impersonal account of grace, there is no implied constraint in John Bradford's freedom to pursue virtue, although ill-fortune may deprive him of successful achievement of that virtue.

The price, however, of removing the tension between the concept of grace and the pursuit of virtue is so to modify the concept of grace that its effects seem little different from the effects of a random and mechanistic throwing of dice. That rain should fall equally unpurposively upon the just and the unjust as an element of our perception of grace may leave us as free to pursue virtue as when confronted by Shakespeare's slings and arrows, but it does not leave us with much of a concept of grace. Of course, however, we must remind ourselves that this particular account of grace (if such it be) is an ultimate limiting conception at one furthest end of the spectrum, and is hardly therefore a real test of the effectiveness of the concept. . . . Let us consider the account which might be given of the concept at the opposing extremity of the spectrum.

To sketch such an account we substitute the personal for the impersonal and the purposive for the mechanistic. This strengthens and enriches the concept of grace immensely by implying a source of the effects of grace which is quite different from the 'source' of outrageous fortune's slings and arrows. Thus for the paraphrase: *But for the absence of outrageous fortune, there goes John Bradford*, we can substitute the following expansion: *But for the action of a personal and purposive God, there goes John Bradford*. Now this has the theological advantage of giving a distinctive account of grace which is certainly not in danger of being confused with fortune, whether outrageous or not. However, there are disadvantages. Two of these relate to the difficulties which arise for our grasp of what freedom to pursue virtue amounts to, and two to the implied concept of God.

The first of these difficulties is whether or not we have in fact only the illusion of freedom, and if this fear is well-grounded, then this conception of the grace of God sets the greatest possible limit to our freedom to pursue virtue. If there be such a God, and if such a God may choose either to act or not to act graciously, then are we merely the small children in the garden, believing ourselves to be freely working out purposes of significance and taking final responsibility for these purposes; or are all of our deeds and purposes subject in the end to the constraints set by and potential intervention of those who know better what is good for us? In such a case, freedom to pursue virtue, which must include freedom to set and pursue specific goals, is deeply in question.

The second related difficulty also concerning our concept of freedom is raised by the very idea of a purposive and gracious God. If such a gracious purposive being exists, how much freedom do we have within his purposes? Is it sufficient to formulate moral goals and to pursue them? If so, why is that apportioning of freedom not sufficient to achieve those goals? Or if it is sufficient what need do we have of the (interventionist) grace of God? If God's grace is to be seen in the initial provision of freedom, rather than in some interventionist form ('special' grace), then why is that grace relevant to the distinction between John Bradford and the criminals whom he observed?

The difficulties raised by this account of grace for the concept of God are well-known and closely correlated to the above points about freedom. All of these points were made most effectively by Hume in his *Dialogues Concerning Natural Religion* and therefore I shall note rather than dwell upon them. The first is that such a gracious purposive God seems to be rather selective in his interventions. Why should John Bradford have the support of the grace of God, but apparently not so the poor wretches who provoked the chilled *frisson* in his heart? The second difficulty is that if we depend upon appeal to concepts such as purposiveness and personalness to distinguish the grace of God from 'slings and arrows', then the logic of the situation is that we give content to the distinction by increasing the anthropomorphism and Philo's reminder to Cleanthes is relevant. The force of the distinction is stronger, the closer the analogy between divine purposiveness and human purposiveness. Weaken the comparison, and you diminish the cogency of the argument:

Now Cleanthes, said Philo, with an air of alacrity and triumph, mark the consequences. *First*, by this method of reasoning you remove all claims to infinity in any of the attributes of deity . . .

Secondly, you have no reason, on your Theory, for ascribing perfection to the Deity . . . (David Hume, *Dialogues*, Section 5)

Leonardo Boff, *Liberating Grace*, ET Maryknoll, NY, Orbis, 1990, pp. 15, 17

The chief problem in discussions about grace lies in the effort to maintain the proper balance between the two poles involved: God and human beings. Grace is essentially encounter and relationship. It is God communicating himself and human beings opening themselves up. When we maintain this polarity then we can properly ponder and talk about grace.

Under the conditioning of cultural factors, the history of theological reflection has oscillated between one pole and the other. Greek Christian tradition put the emphasis on God and on deification. Latin Christian tradition put the emphasis on the human experience of sinfulness and on grace as the justification of human beings. Both traditions ran the risk of overlooking the specific feature of grace as encounter. As a result they reified grace. On the one side grace was God in himself (uncreated grace) who took in humans and divinized them. On the other side, grace was the effect of God's love in humans (created grace), an ontological effect that alters humans.

The latter view led people to develop their views of created grace. What was its nature? It is an accident, said the medieval theologians and the neo-scholastics, because it is something added to the substance of human beings. It itself cannot be a substance because then it would be another thing alongside the human being and could not modify the human substance. Yet in this case the accident, grace, is more noble than the substance, the human being. Isn't that very odd?

Such problems arose because of the inadequacy of the theoretical tools used to comprehend the reality in question. A more satisfactory approach had to be found. The theoretical armory of the medieval scholastics did not allow them to deal with the dimensions of encounter and dialogue that are part and parcel of the reality of grace. Grace implies the alteration of both God and humans. It establishes an encounter, a dialogue, and a flow of mutual love. Both are vulnerable because grace operates in the framework of freedom, where there can be a flowering of the unexpected or degeneration on the part of human beings. Humans can close up in themselves and reject love. Thus grace reveals the authentic structure of human beings. On the one hand, they embody a native desire for God; on the other hand, they can also reject this God.

In the reality known as grace we find an opposition, in the original sense of that word (*ob-pono*). Two things are placed before each other, and so there is a relationship involved in grace. In the history of theological reflection on the experience of grace, people mistakenly came to express this opposition in terms of a straight clash between the two poles. That is what happened in the interminable discussions about nature and grace. Theologians stressed the part of God sometimes and the part of human beings at other times.

But grace does not refer to God solely as an infinite nature closed up in its own omnipotent autonomy. Nor does it refer solely to human beings as natures closed up in their own natural self-sufficiency. Described in terms of nature, these two images of God and the human being do not succeed in communicating the dialogical reality of God and humans, which is characterized by freedom, gratuitousness, and an openness to the other. Grace is not just God, not just the human being. It is the encounter of the two, each giving of self and opening up to the other.

John Oman, *Grace and Personality*, London, Collins, 1960, pp. 157–9, 161–2

If grace as direct power, which proves itself omnipotent as it is irresistible, is God's only adequate way of working, the manifest sins and errors of mankind would seem to show that he is as parsimonious in his exercise of it as the Pope of his infallibility. Why, if it is only a matter of God moulding us to his will by the word of his power, should there be difficulty so great and failure so deplorable?

Our will obviously must have some place, if only to explain error and evil. But when we seek, alongside of grace as direct power, room for will as another direct power, we find ourselves trying to conceive that God makes us free by compulsion, while, yet, we are free only as we are not compelled, that God, by the might of his hand, shapes our thinking to truth, our feeling to purity and our wills to good, while, yet, except as we see for ourselves nothing is true, except as our own hearts reverence nothing is pure, except as our own purpose is consecrated nothing is good.

When our doing and God's doing thus become irreconcilable mechanical opposites, and we find ourselves, not only in conflict with experience, but introducing absurdities into it, we ought surely to realise that we have missed our way.

Yet it is followed blindly and persistently, partly from the mechanical nature of our thinking, which tends to reduce all explanations to the appearance of a law of motion, even in the personal sphere where it is wholly misleading, and partly from the lack of practical harmony in our whole dealing with experience, whereby our faiths and our purposes are actually in continual conflict. We constantly look at life religiously and morally, as through a binocular out of focus. At best we dimly feel these worlds are one, though we cannot help seeing them apart even when we look with both eyes; at worst we shut one eye and look morally, and then open that and shut the other and look religiously. Then we say very sagely, room must be found for both worlds. Life, we say, is not a circle but an ellipse with two foci. God is grace, but he is also power – as if the whole question were not whether the ultimate power is gracious; or God reveals himself in Christ, but also in Nature – as if the whole question of Christ were not how Nature is to be interpreted by the purpose of God; or God is love, but he is also justice – as if the whole question of the government of God did not concern a righteous love; or God speaks in his Word, but also in conscience – as if there were any word of God not manifested to every man's conscience or any conscience apart from the manifestation of the mind of God; or there is the problem of the individual, but there is also the problem of the Kingdom of God, meaning by that, compromises and adjustments between the claims of institutions and the vagaries of their members – as though the whole issue of religion did not concern social persons who only find their own kingdom as they discover God's.

The task of theology is not to effect some kind of working compromise between the two tubes of the binocular, but to find their proper adjustment to one clear field of vision, so that we shall not be moral and religious, but shall so depend upon God as to have in all things moral independence, till our religion becomes morality and our morality religion.

God is not concerned first with good gifts, but with right giving as measured by right receiving. Grace, that means, is never a mere direct line of power, passing through us with impersonal directness, as light through window-glass, but is a curve of patient, personal wisdom, encircling and embracing us and all our concerns. And with that curve a true theology is wholly occupied.

Grace has always a convex side towards God, and a concave side towards man. Taken separately, they are contradictory and opposite, but, united, they are as perfectly one as the convex and concave sides in one line. As acts of grace and acts of will, they are sheer conflicting forces; in the gracious relation to us of the Father of our spirits, their harmony is the essential expression of our fellowship. Yet, the harmony of love, not of absorption, of personal agreement, not of pantheistic oneness, can be won only as we realise the contradiction and see how God overcomes it, by accepting it.

Every right doctrine of grace, therefore, starts from the conflict between us and God as individuals which, just because it belongs to our power as persons to maintain, God's indirect personal dealing with us alone can overcome.

. . .

All doctrines of grace, being doctrines of love, and not of power, must accept these mechanical opposites, which are there so long as our will is set in one direction and God's in another. They may neither be ignored nor overridden, but, on the contrary, it is of the essence of a gracious personal relation to be wholly determined by them. It may not take the easy road of might, for, then, instead of being rid of the mechanical opposition, the relation between God and man becomes wholly mechanical, as between forces not persons. The very business of a doctrine of grace, on the contrary, is to show how grace steadfastly maintains a relation between God and his children, wherein we remain persons even as he is a person, and have moral independence even as he has, an independence which we only perfectly achieve, as we attain a perfect trust in our Father, whereby we can serve him joyously, as love can alone be served, in his children.

An account of the way of the working of God's gracious relation to us, therefore, is just an account of these opposites, which, so long as they are opposed mechanically, are irreconcilable contradictions, and of how love overcomes them by a personal dealing which turns them into the perfect harmony of unbroken peace and unceasing purpose of good. The problem is how to set forth the doctrines of grace, so that salvation shall not be either God's working or our own, or, in part, God's gift, and, in part, our own achievement, but, from its beginning in penitence to its completion in the possession of eternal life, be, all of it, at once of God's giving and of our own achieving, at once of God's working in us the willing and the doing, and of our working out our own salvation with a fear and trembling which is at once a recognition of a reality and the imperfection of our task, and a trust in God's as alone making it perfect and secure.

4.5 God's work alone?

Karl Barth, *Dogmatics in Outline,* **ET London, SCM, 1966, pp. 16, 17, 18**

I believe in, *credo in*, means that I am not alone. In our glory and in our misery we men are not alone. God comes to meet us and as our Lord and Master he comes to our aid. We live and act and suffer, in good and in bad days, in our perversity and in our rightness, in this confrontation with God. I am not alone, but God meets me; one way or other, I am in all circumstances in company with him. That is, I believe in God, the Father, the Son, and the Holy Spirit. This meeting with God is the meeting with the word of grace which he has spoken in Jesus Christ. Faith speaks of God, the Father, the Son and the Holy Spirit, as him who meets us, as the object of faith, and says of this God that he is one in himself, has become single in himself for us and has become single once more in the eternal decree, explicated in time, of his free, unowed, unconditional love for man, for all men, in the counsel of his grace. God is gracious to us – this is what the Confession of the Father, Son and Holy Spirit, says. This includes the fact that of ourselves we cannot achieve, have not achieved, and shall not achieve a togetherness with him; that we have not deserved that he should be our God, have no power of disposal and no rights over him, but that with unowed kindness, in the freedom of his majesty, he resolved of his own self to be man's God, our God. He *tells* us that this is so. God's telling us, 'I am gracious to you', is the Word of God, the central concept of all Christian thinking. The Word of God is the word of his grace. And if you ask me where we hear this Word of God, I can only point to himself, who enables us to hear it, and reply with the mighty centre of the Confession, with the second article, that the Word of God's grace in which he meets us is called Jesus Christ, the Son of God and Son of man, true God and true Man, Immanuel, God with us in this One. Christian faith is the meeting with this 'Immanuel', the meeting with Jesus Christ and in him with the living Word of God. In calling Holy Scripture the Word of God (and we so call it, because it is so), we mean by it Holy Scripture as the witness of the prophets and the apostles to this one Word of God, to Jesus, the man out of Israel, who is God's Christ, our Lord and King in eternity. And in confessing this, in venturing to call the Church's proclamation God's Word, we must be understood to mean the proclamation of Jesus Christ, of him who is true God and true Man for our good. In him God meets us. And when we say, I believe *in* God, the concrete meaning is that I believe in the Lord Jesus Christ.

I have described this meeting as a gift. It is a meeting in which men become free to hear God's Word. The gift and the becoming free belong to each other. The gift is the gift of a freedom, of the great freedom in which all other freedoms are included. I really wish I might succeed . . . in restoring to your favour this much misused and yet most noble word 'freedom', starting from this centre or core outwards. Freedom is God's great gift, the gift of meeting with him. Why a gift, and why a gift of freedom? What it means is that this meeting of which the Creed speaks does not take place in vain. It rests not upon a human possibility and human initiative, nor on the fact that we men bear in us a capacity to meet God, to hear his Word. Were we to reckon up for ourselves what we men are capable of, we should strive in vain to discover anything which might be termed a disposition towards the Word of God. Without any possibility on our side God's great possibility comes into view, making possible what is impossible from our side. It is God's gift, God's free gift, not prepared for by anything on our side, *if* we meet him and in meeting with him hear his Word. The Creed of the Father, Son and Holy Spirit speaks in all three articles of a nature and work absolutely new to us men, inaccessible and inconceivable to us. And as this nature and work of God the Father, the Son and the Holy Spirit is his free grace towards us, it is grace all over again if our eyes and ears are opened to this grace.

. . .

I give praise and thanks for the fact that I am elect, that I am called, that my Lord has made me free for himself. In that confidence I believe. That which I do in believing is the only thing left me, to which I have been invited, to which I have been made free by him who can do what I can neither begin nor accomplish of myself. I make use of the gift in which God has given me himself. I breathe, and now I breathe joyfully and freely in the freedom which I have not taken to myself, which I have not sought nor found by myself, but in which God has come to me and adopted me.

Karl Barth, *Deliverance to the Captives*, ET London, SCM, 1961, pp. 39, 40

Because we are saved by no other than Jesus Christ, we are saved *by grace*. This means that we did not deserve to be saved. What we deserved would be quite different. We cannot secure salvation for ourselves. . . . [W]e cannot produce our salvation. No one can be proud of being saved. Each one can only fold his hands in great lowliness of heart and be thankful like a child. Consequently we shall never possess salvation as our property. We may only receive it as a gift over and over again, with hands outstretched. '*By grace* you have been saved!' [*Ephesians 2:5, 8*]. This means constantly to look away from ourselves to God and to the man on the cross where this truth is revealed. This truth is ever anew to be believed and to be grasped by faith. To believe means to look to Jesus Christ and to God and to trust that there is the truth for us, for our lives, for the life of all men.

John Oman, *Grace and Personality*, London, Collins, 1960, pp. 25–7

God does not conduct his rivers, like arrows, to the sea. The ruler and compass are only for finite mortals who labour, by taking thought, to overcome their limitations, and are not for the Infinite mind. The expedition demanded by man's small power and short day produces the canal, but nature, with a beneficent and picturesque circumambulancy, the work of a more spacious and less precipitate mind, produces the river. Why should we assume that, in all the rest of his ways, he rejoices in the river, but, in religion, can use no adequate method save the canal?

The defence of the infallible is the defence of the canal against the river, of the channel blasted through the rock against the basin dug by an element which swerves at a pebble or a firmer clay. And the question is whether God ever does override the human spirit in that direct way, and whether we ought to conceive either of his spirit or of ours after a fashion that could make it possible. Would such irresistible might as would save us from all error and compel us into right action be in accord either with God's personality or with ours?

. . .

When we turn from argument to reality, there is little to show that either truth or righteousness ever came by way of irresistible might. Progress ever winds slowly forward, fretting at every obstacle and constantly returning upon its path, never working with absolute things, but always with the struggle of human thought and purpose. The long sorrowful experience of the ages seems to show that the last thing God thinks of doing is to drive mankind, with resistless rein, on the highway of righteousness.

All infallibilities presuppose an idea of grace mechanically irresistible. But a direct force controlling persons as things is no personal relation between God and man; and the religion which rests on it does nothing to maintain the supreme interest of religion, which is the worth of persons over things, of moral values over material forces. God might so act upon men and still be a person, but there would be nothing personal in his acting; he might even care for each individual, but it would not be as a soul thinking its own thoughts and acting according to its own thinking; and the whole method has to be restricted to special spheres of grace, else it would not be an explanation of the world in any essential way different from heartless, rational cosmic process. May it not be that we shall not find less of God in life and not find his operation less adequate to our spiritual needs, because we discover his method to be patient enough to pass round by way of persuasion and education through our errors and failures?

Joint Declaration on the Doctrine of Justification: The Lutheran World Federation and The Roman Catholic Church, ET Grand Rapids, MI, Eerdmans, 2000, pp. 10–14, 16–17, 20, 25

The present *Joint Declaration* has this intention: namely, to show that on the basis of their dialogue the subscribing Lutheran churches and the Roman Catholic Church are now able to articulate a common understanding of our justification by God's grace through faith in Christ.

. . .

Our common way of listening to the word of God in Scripture has led to . . . new insights. Together we hear the gospel that 'God so loved the world that he gave his only Son, so that everyone who believes in him may not perish but may have eternal life' (John 3:16).

. . .

Justification is the forgiveness of sins (cf. Romans 3:23–25; Acts 13:39; Luke 18:14), liberation from the dominating power of sin and death (Romans 5:12–21) and from the curse of the law (Galatians 3:10–14). It is acceptance into communion with God – already now, but then fully in God's coming kingdom (Romans 5:1–2). It unites with Christ and with his death and resurrection (Romans 6:5). It occurs in the reception of the Holy Spirit in baptism and incorporation into the one body (Romans 8:1–2, 9–10; 1 Corinthians 12:12–13). All this is from God alone, for Christ's sake, by grace, through faith in 'the gospel of God's Son' (Romans 1:1–3).

. . .

All people are called by God to salvation in Christ. Through Christ alone are we justified, when we receive this salvation in faith. Faith is itself God's gift through the Holy Spirit, who works through Word and Sacrament in the community of believers. . . . We also share the conviction that the message of justification directs us in a special way toward the heart of the New Testament witness to God's saving action in Christ: it tells us that because we are sinners our new life is solely due to the forgiving and renewing mercy that God imparts as a gift and we receive in faith, and never can merit in any way.

. . .

Justification takes place solely by God's grace. Because Catholics and Lutherans confess this together, it is true that:

When Catholics say that persons 'cooperate' in preparing for and accepting justification by consenting to God's justifying action, they see such personal consent as itself an effect of grace, not as an action arising from innate human abilities.

. . .

This new personal relation to God is grounded totally in God's graciousness and remains constantly dependent on the salvific and creative working of this gracious God, who remains true to himself, so that one can rely upon him. Thus justifying grace never becomes a human possession to which one could appeal over against God.

. . .

When Catholics affirm the 'meritorious' character of good works, they wish to say that, according to the biblical witness, a reward in heaven is promised to these works. Their intention is to emphasize the responsibility of persons for their actions, not to contest the character of those works as gifts, or far less to deny that justification always remains the unmerited gift of grace.

Topics for discussion

1 Give an account of the Christian understanding of grace. How might it be challenged?
2 Trace the relationships between (a) grace and freedom, and (b) sin and grace.
3 What difficulties face the claim that there is a distinctive experience that can be labelled an experience of grace?
4 Discuss the advantages and disadvantages of understanding grace as personal.
5 What do you understand by claim that grace is 'the fundamental form of God's relation to the creature' (Colin Gunton). Where does this leave other Christian doctrines?

Acknowledgements

The Scripture quotations contained herein are from The New Revised Standard Version of the Bible, Anglicized Edition, copyright © 1989, 1995 by the Division of Christian Education of the National Council of the Churches of Christ in the United States of America, and are used by permission. All rights reserved. To SCM-Canterbury Press Ltd for quotations from *Finding and Following* by Helen Oppenheimer; SCM-Canterbury Press Ltd for quotations from *Providence* by Michael J. Langford; SCM-Canterbury Press Ltd for quotations from *God's Action in the World* by Maurice Wiles; *Modern Theology* for a quotation from 'Farrer, Wiles and the Casual Joint' by Vincent Brümmer in *Modern Theology*, 8 (1) (© Blackwell Publishers Ltd, 1992); Blackwell Publishers Ltd for quotations from 'Divine Action' by Thomas F. Tracy in *A Companion to the Philosophy of Religion* edited by P. L. Quinn and C. Taliaferro; Paternoster Press for a quotation from *The Fall of a Sparrow* by Vernon White; T & T Clark International for quotations from 'How to Think about Divine Action' by William Alston and from 'God and Symbolic Action' by David Brown in *Divine Action* edited by Brian Hebblethwaite and Edward Henderson; Church House Publishing for quotations from *We Believe in God: A Report by the Doctrine Commission of the General Synod of the Church of England* (1987); HarperCollins Publishers Ltd for a quotation from *The World and God* by H. H. Farmer (Collins 1963); SCM-Canterbury Press Ltd and the University of Chicago Press for quotations from *Systematic Theology Volume 1* by Paul Tillich; HarperCollins Publishers Ltd for a quotation from *Divine Action* by Keith Ward (reprinted by HarperCollins Publishers Ltd ©) (Originally published by Collins, 1990); Penguin UK for a quotation from *The Gospel of St John* by John Marsh © John Marsh; Penn State University Press for a quotation from *The Fear of Freedom: A Study of Miracles in the Roman Imperial Church* by Rowan A. Greer (University Park, PA: The Pennsylvania State University Press, 1989), pp. 44–5 copyright 1989 by The Pennsylvania State University. SCM-Canterbury Press for quotations from *God, Miracle and the Church of*

England by David E. Jenkins; Oxford University Press for quotations from 'Of Miracles' by David Hume in *An Enquiry Concerning the Human Understanding*, 1777, section X (reprinted in L. A. Selby-Bigge's edition, 1902); Continuum Books for a quotation from 'Approaches to Prayer' by Johann Baptist Metz in *The Courage to Pray* edited by J. B. Metz and K. Rahner (Burns and Oates 1980); SCM-Canterbury Press Ltd for quotations from *Prayer and Providence: A Background Study* by Peter Baelz; Oxford University Press for a quotation from *Essays in the Philosophy of Religion* by H. H. Price; Ashgate Publishing for a quotation from © *Theology and Psychology* by Fraser Watts, 2002; SCM-Canterbury Press Ltd for quotation from *What are we doing When We Pray? A Philosophical Enquiry* by Vincent Brümmer; The C. S. Lewis Company for quotations from *Miracles: A Preliminary Study* by C. S. Lewis copyright © C. S. Lewis Pte. Ltd 1947, 1960 (originally published by Harper Collins, 1974); Routledge and Kegan Paul for quotations from *God and the Soul* by Peter Geach; Peeters Publishers for quotations from 'Prayer and Providence' by Paul Helm in *Christian Faith and Philosophical Theology* edited by G. Van den Brink, L. Van den Brom and M. Sarot (Kok Pharos 1992); HarperCollins Publishers Ltd for *The Power of Prayer in Relation to Outward Circumstances* by Friedrich Schleiermacher; SPCK for a quotation from *Our Understanding of Prayer* by Ian T. Ramsey; Routledge and Kegan Paul for a quotation from *The Concept of Prayer* by D. Z. Philips; Epworth Press for a quotation from Doxology: *The Praise of God in Worship, Doctrine and Life* by Geoffrey Wainwright (© Epworth Press 1980); SCM-Canterbury Press Ltd for a quotation from *The Cost of Discipleship* (ET London) by Dietrich Bonhoeffer; Darton Longman & Todd for *Theological Investigations* Vol. III by Karl Rahner; Oxford University Press for a quotation from 'Butler and Deism' by David Brown in *Joseph Butler's Moral and Religious Thought: Tercentenary Essays* edited by Christopher Cunliffe © Christopher Cunliffe 1992; T & T Clark International for quotations from 'God and Freedom' by Stewart R. Sutherland in *God and Freedom: Essays in Historical and Systematic Theology* by Colin E. Gunton (Edinburgh, T & T Clark 1995); Orbis Books for quotations from *Liberating Grace* by Leonardo Boff, Maryknoll, NY, Orbis 1990; SCM-Canterbury Press Ltd for quotations from *Dogmatics in Outline* (ET London) by Karl Barth; SCM-Canterbury Press Ltd for quotations from *Deliverance to the Captives* (ET London) by Karl Barth; HarperCollins Publishers Ltd for *Grace and Personality* by John Oman; Eerdmans for quotations from *Joint Declaration on the Doctrine of Justification: The Lutheran World Federation and the Roman Catholic Church* (ET Grand Rapids, MI, 2000).

Further reading

Introductory and general

Astley, J. (2000) *God's World*, London, Darton, Longman & Todd, Chs 2, 3 and 4.

Astley, J., Brown, D. and Loades, A. (eds) (2003) *Creation: A Reader*, London, T & T Clark.

Astley, J., Brown, D. and Loades, A. (eds) (2004) *Science and Religion: A Reader*, London, T & T Clark International.

Davies, B. (1985) *Thinking about God*, London, Chapman, Chs 2 and 11.

Farmer, H. H. (1963) *The World and God: A Study of Prayer, Providence and Miracle in Christian Experience*, London, Collins.

Farrer, A. (1964) *Saving Belief: A Discussion*, London, Hodder & Stoughton, pp. 37–58.

Farrer, A. (1966) *A Science of God?* London, Bles.

Geach, P. (1969) *God and the Soul*, London, Routledge & Kegan Paul.

Hebblethwaite, B. and Anderson, E. (eds) (1990) *Divine Action*, Edinburgh, T & T Clark.

Langford, M. J. (1981) *Providence*, London, SCM.

Lucas, J. R. (1976) *Freedom and Grace*, London, SPCK.

Meynell, H. (1971) *God and the World*, London, SPCK.

Morris, T. V. (ed.) (1988) *Divine and Human Action: Essays in the Metaphysics of Theism*, Ithaca, NY, Cornell University Press.

Oppenheimer, H. (1994) *Finding and Following: Talking with Children About God*, London, SCM, Chs 6, 7 and 8.

Pailin, D. A. (1989) *God and the Processes of Reality: Foundations of a Credible Theism*, London, Routledge.

Purtill, R. L. (1978) *Thinking About Religion: A Philosophical Introduction to Religion*, Englewood Cliffs, NJ, Prentice-Hall, Ch. 5.

Quinn, P. L. and Taliaferro, C. (eds) (1997) *A Companion to Philosophy of Religion*, Oxford, Blackwell, Chs 37, 38, 46, 72 and 73.

Southgate, C., *et al.* (eds.) (1999) *God, Humanity and the Cosmos: A Textbook in Science and Religion*, Edinburgh, T & T Clark, Ch. 7.

Thomas, O. C. (ed.) (1983) *God's Activity in the World: The Contemporary Problem*, Chico, CA, Scholars Press.

Tracy, T. F. (ed.) (1994) *The God Who Acts: Philosophical and Theological Explorations*, University Park, PA, Pennsylvania State University Press.

Vardy, P. (1990) *The Puzzle of God*, London, Collins, Chs 14 to 17.

Ward, K (1990) *Divine Action*, London, Collins.

1 Providence

Alston, W. P. (1989) *Divine Nature and Human Language: Essays in Philosophical Theology*, Ithaca, NY, Cornell University Press, Chs 4 and 10.

Bartholomew, D. J. (1984) *God of Chance*, London, SCM.

Brümmer, V. (1992) *Speaking of a Personal God: An Essay in Philosophical Theology*, Cambridge, Cambridge University Press, Ch. 5.

Farrer, A. (1967) *Faith and Speculation: An Essay in Philosophical Theology*, London, A & C Black, Chs IX to XI.

Geach, P. T. (1977) *Providence and Evil*, Cambridge, Cambridge University Press.

Gorringe, T. J. (1991) *God's Theatre: A Theology of Providence*, London, SCM.

Goulder, M. and Hick, J. (1983) *Why Believe in God?*, London, SCM, Chs 4 and 5.

Hebblethwaite, B. L. (1978) 'Providence and Divine Action', *Religious Studies*, 14, pp. 223–36.

Helm, P. (1993) *The Providence of God*, Downers Grove, IL, InterVarsity Press.

Kaufman, G. D. (1972) *God the Problem*, Cambridge, MA, Harvard University Press.

Macmurray, J. (1957, 1969) *The Self as Agent*, London, Faber and Faber.

Peacocke, A. (1993) *Theology for a Scientific Age: Being and Becoming – Natural, Divine and Human*, London, SCM, Ch. 9.

Polkinghorne, J. (1989) *Science and Providence*, London, SPCK.

Swinburne, R. (1998) *Providence and the Problem of Evil*, Oxford, Oxford University Press.

Tracy, T. F. (1984) *God, Action, and Embodiment*, Grand Rapids, MI, Eerdmans.

Ward, K. (1992) *Holding Fast to God*, London, SPCK, Ch. 8.

White, V. (1985) *The Fall of a Sparrow: A Concept of Special Divine Action*, Exeter, Paternoster.

Wiles, M. (1986) *God's Action in the World*, London, SCM, Chs 2 and 3.

Wiles, M. (ed.) (1969) *Providence*, London, SPCK.

2 Miracles

Eaton, J. C. (1985) 'The Problem of Miracles and the Paradox of Double Agency', *Modern Theology*, 1, 3, pp. 211–22.

Gaskin, J. C. A. (1988) *Hume's Philosophy of Religion*, London, Macmillan, Ch. 8.

Geivett, R. D. and Habermas, G. R. (eds) (1997) *In Defence of Miracles: A Comprehensive Case for God's Action in History*, Leicester, InterVarsity Press.

Greer, R. A. (1989) *The Fear of Freedom: A Study of Miracles in the Roman Imperial Church*, University Park, PA, Pennsylvania State University Press.

Gwynne, P. (1996) *Special Divine Action: Key Issues in the Contemporary Debate (1965–1995)*, Rome, Gregorian University Press.

Houston, J. (1994) *Reported Miracles: A Critique of Hume*, Cambridge, Cambridge University Press.

Hume, D. (1748, many editions) 'Of Miracles', in *An Enquiry Concerning Human Understanding*, Section X.

Jenkins, D. (1987) *God, Miracle and the Church of England*, London, SCM.

Keller, E. and Keller, M.-L. (1969) *Miracles in Dispute*, ET London, SCM.

Lewis, C. S. (1947, 1974) *Miracles*, London, HarperCollins; (1996) New York, Simon & Schuster.

Moule, C. F. D. (ed.) (1965) *Miracles: Cambridge Studies in their Philosophy and History*, London, Mowbray.

Mullin, R. B. (1996) *Miracles and the Modern Religious Imagination*, New Haven, CT, Yale University Press.

Peterson, M., Hasker, W., Reichenbach, B. and Basinger, D. (1991) *Reason and Religious Belief: An Introduction to the Philosophy of Religion*, New York, Oxford University Press, Ch. 9.

Swinburne, R. (1970) *The Concept of Miracle*, London, Macmillan.

Swinburne, R. (ed.) (1989) *Miracles*, New York, Macmillan.

Ward, B. (1982) *Miracles and the Medieval World: Theory, Record and Event 1000–1215*, London, Scolar Press.

Ward, K. (1985) 'Miracles and Testimony', *Religious Studies*, 21, 2, pp. 131–45.

Wolterstorff, N. (1995) *Divine Discourse: Philosophical Reflections on the Claim that God Speaks*, Cambridge, Cambridge University Press, Ch. 7.

3 Prayer

Baelz, P. (1968) *Prayer and Providence: A Background Study*, London, SCM.

Baelz, P. (1982) *Does God Answer Prayer?*, London, Darton, Longman & Todd.

Barth, K. (1965) *Evangelical Theology: An Introduction*, ET London, Collins, Ch. 14.

Basinger, D. (1983) 'Why Petition an Omnipotent, Omniscient, Wholly Good God?', *Religious Studies* 19, pp. 25–42.

Basinger, D. (1995) 'Petitionary Prayer: A Response to Murray and Meyers', *Religious Studies*, 31, pp. 475–84.

Brümmer, V. (1984) *What Are We Doing When We Pray?*, London, SCM.

Helm, P. (1992) 'Prayer and Providence', in G. van den Brink, L. van den Brom and M. Sarot (eds) *Christian Faith and Philosophical Theology*, Kampen, The Netherlands, Kok Pharos, pp. 103–15.

Henderson, E. H. (1985) 'Austin Farrer and D. Z. Phillips on Lived Faith, Prayer, and Divine Reality', *Modern Theology* 1, 3, pp. 223–43.

Law, J. T. (1995) 'Questions People Ask 3. Prayer: Problem or Possibility?', *The Expository Times*, 107, 1, pp. 4–10.

McCabe, H. (2002) *God Still Matters*, London, Continuum, Chs 6 and 19.

Murray, M. J. and Meyers, K. (1994) 'Ask and It Will Be Given to You', *Religious Studies*, 30, pp. 311–30.

Phillips, D. Z. (1965) *The Concept of Prayer*, London, Routledge & Kegan Paul.

Rahner, K. (1975) *Christian at the Crossroads*, ET London, Burns & Oates, Part II, Chs 2 and 3.

Ramsey, I. T. (1971) *Our Understanding of Prayer*, London, SPCK.

Stump, E. (1999) 'Petitionary Prayer', reprinted in E. Stump and M. J. Murray (eds) *Philosophy of Religion: The Big Questions*, Oxford, Blackwell, pp. 353–66.

Tilley, T. W. (1991) ' "Lord, I Believe: Help My Unbelief": Prayer Without Belief', *Modern Theology*, 7, 3, pp. 239–47.

Wallis, I. G. (1995) 'Jesus, Human Being and the Praxis of Intercession: Towards a Biblical Perspective', *Scottish Journal of Theology*, 48, 2, pp. 225–50.

Watts, F. (ed.) (2001) *Perspectives on Prayer*, London, SPCK.

4 Grace

Anderson, H. G., Murphy, T. A. and Burgess, J. A. (eds) (1985) *Justification by Faith: Lutherans and Catholics in Dialogue*, Minneapolis, MN, Augsburg.

Boff, L. (1979) *Liberating Grace*, ET Maryknoll, Orbis.

Brümmer, V. (1992) *Speaking of a Personal God: An Essay in Philosophical Theology*, Cambridge, Cambridge University Press, Ch. 3.

Condon, K., CM (1967) 'The Biblical Doctrine of Original Sin', *Irish Theological Quarterly*, 34, pp. 20–36.

Daly, G. (1994) 'Original Sin', in M. Walsh (ed.) *Commentary on the Catechism of the Catholic Church*, London, Chapman, pp. 97–111.

Day, A. J. (1998) 'Adam, Anthropology and the Genesis Record – Taking Genesis Seriously in the Light of Contemporary Science', *Science and Christian Belief*, 10, 2, pp. 115–143.

Duffy, S. J. (1993) *The Dynamics of Grace: Perspectives in Theological Anthropology*, Collegeville, MI, The Liturgical Press.

Dunn, J. D. G. and Suggate, A. M. (1993) *The Justice of God: A Fresh Look at the Old Doctrine of Justification by Faith*, Carlisle, Paternoster.

Farrer, A. (1967) *Faith and Speculation: An Essay in Philosophical Theology*, London, A. & C. Black, Ch. IV.

Farrer, A. (1972) *Reflective Faith: Essays in Philosophical Theology*, London, SPCK, pp. 192–9.

Farrer, A. (1976) *Interpretation and Belief*, London, SPCK, pp. 95–100.

Fransen, P., SJ (1965) *Divine Grace and Man*, ET New York, New American Library.

Gleason, R. W., SJ (1962) *Grace*, London, Sheed and Ward.

Gunton, C. E. (ed.) (1995) *God and Freedom: Essays in Historical and Systematic Theology*, Edinburgh, T & T Clark.

Haight, R. (1979) *The Language and Experience of Grace*, New York, Paulist.

Haight, R. (1991) 'Sin and Grace', in F. S. Fiorenza and J. P. Galvin (eds) *Systematic Theology: Roman Catholic Perspectives*, Vol. 2, Minneapolis, MN, Fortress, pp. 77–141.

Küng, H. (1981) *Justification: The Doctrine of Karl Barth and a Catholic Reflection*, London, Burns & Oates.

Lane, A. N. S. (2002) *Justification by Faith in Catholic-Protestant Dialogue: An Evangelical Assessment*, London, T & T Clark.

McGrath, A. E. (1986) *Iustitia Dei: A History of the Christian Doctrine of Justification*, 2 vols, Cambridge, Cambridge University Press.

Mitchell, B. (1957) 'The Grace of God', in B. Mitchell (ed.) *Faith and Logic:*

Oxford Essays in Philosophical Theology, London, George Allen & Unwin, 1957, Ch. VI.

Moore, S. (1998) 'Getting the Fall Right', *The Downside Review*, 116, 404, pp. 213–26.

Oman, J. (1960) *Grace and Personality*, London, Collins.

Oppenheimer, H. (1973) *Incarnation and Immanence*, London, Hodder & Stoughton, Ch. 10.

Rahner, K. (1961) *Theological Investigations 1: God, Christ, Mary and Grace*, ET London, Darton, Longman & Todd, Ch. 9.

Rahner, K. (1963) *Theological Investigations 2: Man in the Church*, ET London, Darton, Longman & Todd, pp. 119–27.

Rahner, K. (1963) *Nature and Grace and Other Essays*, ET London, Sheed and Ward, Part 1.

Ward, K. (1992) *Holding Fast to God*, London, SPCK, Ch. 9.

Ward, K. (1998) *Religion and Human Nature*, Oxford, Oxford University Press.

Wiles, M. (1974) *The Remaking of Christian Doctrine*, London, SCM, Ch. 5.

Yarnold, E., SJ (1974) *The Second Gift: A Study of Grace*, Slough, St. Paul.

Index of subjects

Index of names